T0154336

EXPLORE

TORONTO & ONTARIO

PLAN & BOOK
YOUR TAILOR-MADE TRIP

BRAZIL CHILE ECUADOR

TAILOR-MADE TRIPS & UNIQUE EXPERIENCES CREATED BY LOCAL TRAVEL EXPERTS AT INSIGHTGUIDES.COM/HOLIDAYS

Insight Guides has been inspiring travellers with high-quality travel content for over 45 years. As well as our popular guidebooks, we now offer the opportunity to book tailor-made private trips completely personalised to your needs and interests. By connecting with one of our local experts, you will directly benefit from their expertise and local know-how, helping you create memories that will last a lifetime.

HOW INSIGHTGUIDES.COM/HOLIDAYS WORKS

STEP 1
Pick your dream destination and submit an enquiry, or modify an existing itinerary if you prefer.

STEP 2
Fill in a short form, sharing details of your travel plans and preferences with a local expert.

STEP 3
Your local expert will create your personalised itinerary, which you can amend until you are completely satisfied.

STEP 4
Book securely online. Pack your bags and enjoy your holiday! Your local expert will be available to answer questions during your trip.

CONTENTS

Introduction

Directory

Credits

Best Routes

COVID-19 Updates

While travelling in Canada, be sure to heed all local laws, travel advice and hygiene measures. While we've done all we can to make sure this guide is accurate and up to date, be sure to check ahead.

ART LOVERS

Toronto is proud of its top art galleries. Enjoy the Canadian paintings at the Art Gallery of Ontario (route 6) and the stunning ceramics of the Gardiner Museum (route 1). Make time for the intriguing Gallery of Inuit Art (route 5).

RECOMMENDED ROUTES FOR...

ESCAPING THE CROWDS

Cycle or stroll the lovely woods and pond-like lagoons of the Toronto Islands (route 7), or venture further afield to enjoy the wide sunsets of the Lake Huron shoreline (see route 14).

FAMILIES

Families should never feel marooned in Toronto with a hatful of attractions to suit every age – shoot up to the top of the CN Tower (route 3); gawp at the sea life at Ripley's Aquarium of Canada (route 1); or escape the city centre for Toronto Zoo (route 9).

FOODIES

Get those taste buds singing amidst Toronto's army of cafés and restaurants – perhaps nibble a Portuguese custard tart at St Lawrence Market (route 3), wander Chinatown (route 6), or sample the cosmopolitan eateries of Kensington Market (route 6).

HISTORIANS

Anyone interested in Canadian history is spoilt for choice: there are two splendid stockades, Fort York (route 2) and Fort George (route 10), plus the magnificently restored Ste-Marie among the Hurons (route 13).

ISLAND HOPPING

Catch a boat to explore the wild and beautiful Georgian Bay Islands National Park (route 13). Alternatively, cruise the Thousand Islands from Kingston (route 11), or hop on a ferry over to the Toronto Islands (route 7).

VILLAS AND GARDENS

Toronto is graced by a trio of delightful villas: Campbell House (route 5) and Spadina (route 8) are ultra-genteel, whilst the third, Casa Loma (route 8), is all things kitsch. The gardens at Spadina are a real pleasure.

NATURAL WONDERS

No debating what's at the top of this list – it has to be Niagara Falls (route 10), one of the wonders of the world. But also make a beeline for the islet-studded waters of Georgian Bay Islands National Park (route 13).

INTRODUCTION

An introduction to Toronto and Ontario's geography, customs and culture, plus illuminating background information on cuisine, history and what to do when you're there.

St Lawrence Market, the city's best food and drink market

EXPLORE TORONTO & ONTARIO

Fast paced and exciting, Toronto is Canada's biggest city and the capital of the province of Ontario. It lies at the heart of the country's business and finance sectors, but it also packs a real punch when it comes to all things cultural.

From inauspicious beginnings – the first British settlement here was renowned for its cloying muddiness – Toronto has developed into one of the great cities of North America, relatively safe to visit and generally civil in its demeanour. The city is also justifiably proud of its world-class performing arts scene and is something of a beacon for multiculturalism, its distinctive neighbourhoods proclaiming their diversity in a staggering range of restaurants and cultural institutions which are dotted around both Toronto and Ontario.

GEOGRAPHY AND LAYOUT

The sprawling city of **Toronto** radiates out from the northern shore of Lake Ontario, its downtown dominated by a herd of mighty skyscrapers that are themselves overseen by the soaring CN Tower. Indeed, the CN Tower is visible from almost anywhere in the city, unless it's a particularly cloudy day, and Lake Ontario is always south, no matter where you are. Unlike many a North American city, Torontonians don't just

work downtown, but eat, play, and sleep there, making the city centre an especially lively place crowded with restaurants, cafés, bars, stores and theatres. Most of the principal tourist attractions are here as well, from the delights of the Art Gallery of Ontario through to the Hockey Hall of Fame, and you can stroll leisurely from one to another with an occasional trip on a streetcar or the subway to speed things along. Edging downtown are Toronto's most diverse and interesting neighbourhoods, most memorably Kensington Market, Chinatown and Little Italy and you can even hop on a ferry to savour the rustic charms of the Toronto Islands.

The first nine routes we describe in this guidebook, beginning in the centre of Toronto and working their way out, cover all the most appealing attractions and highlight some of the city's most engaging neighbourhoods. Nevertheless, although Toronto dominates proceedings hereabouts, the province of **Ontario** has much to offer – and our final five routes (see Routes 10–14) pick out a string of high spots. The first

The Toronto Music Garden, themed on Bach's Suite No.1 for Unaccompanied Cello

and most obvious target is the thundering waterfalls of **Niagara Falls**, but there are also the historic charms of **Kingston** and the diverting city of **Ottawa**, Canada's capital – and that's not to mention less urban delights, including the wonderful scenery of the **Georgian Bay Islands National Park** and the pretty little towns of the **Lake Huron** shoreline, Bayfield and Goderich. From Toronto, getting to Niagara Falls, Kingston and Ottawa is fairly easy by train or bus, but you will need your own vehicle to reach Georgian Bay and Lake Huron.

HISTORY

The first Europeans to make regular contact with **Ontario**'s Indigenous Iroquois and Algonquin peoples were the French explorers of the seventeenth and eighteenth centuries, most famously Étienne Brûlé and Samuel de Champlain. These early visitors were preoccupied with the fur trade, and it wasn't until the end of the American War of Independence and the immigration of the United Empire Loyalists from New England that mass settlement began. The British parliament responded to this sudden influx by passing the Canada Act, in 1791, which created the provinces of Upper and Lower Canada (respectively Ontario and Québec). Fifty years later, the British went a step further, granting Canada 'responsible government' (broadly democratic government) and reuniting the two provinces in a loose confederation, prefiguring the final union of 1867 when Upper Canada was redesignated Ontario.

Between 1820 and 1850 a further wave of migrants, mostly English, Irish and Scots, made Upper Canada the most populous and prosperous part of Canada. The first capital of Upper Canada was Niagara-on-the-Lake (see page 67), but this was too near the American border for comfort and the province's lieutenant governor, John Graves Simcoe, moved his administration to the relative safety of Toronto in 1793, calling the new settlement York. This pre-eminence was reinforced towards the end of the nineteenth century by the industrialization of the region's larger towns, a process that was underpinned by the discovery of some of the world's richest mineral deposits: in the

---

Covid-19 Updates

In early 2020, Covid-19 swept across the globe, being categorized as a pandemic by the World Health Organization in March 2020. While travelling in Canada, be sure to heed all local laws, travel advice and hygiene measures; flouting these means risking your own health but can also put a strain on local communities and their medical infrastructure. While we've done all we can to make sure this guide is accurate and up to date, permanent closures and changed opening hours are likely in the wake of coronavirus, so be sure to check ahead.

Art Gallery of Ontario, on the threshold of Chinatown

space of twenty years, nickel was found near Sudbury, silver was discovered at Cobalt, gold was located in Red Lake and iron ore was uncovered at Wawa.

DON'T LEAVE TORONTO AND ONTARIO WITHOUT...

Indulging in a treat at the St Lawrence Market. The ultimate market-stall experience, this is where locals stock up on cheeses, sweet pastries, fresh seasonal fruit and produce, as well as imported specialties. Try the peameal bacon sandwich from the Carousel Bakery, a delicious Toronto speciality. See page 38.

Drinking a beer in the Distillery Historic District. Local craft breweries abound in Toronto, but a refreshing brew is especially enjoyed in this reclaimed, cobblestoned, pedestrian-only neighbourhood, where Victorian architecture blends with contemporary industrial design. See page 42.

Heading to the top of the CN Tower. This is Toronto's mascot and the vantage point it offers from the 446.5-metre (1,465ft) -high floor is unforgettable. Try it at night for an alternative perspective or dare to go out along the thrilling EdgeWalk. See page 36.

Strolling through quirky Kensington Market. Popping into the independent boutiques and cutting-edge art galleries of this boho neighbourhood is only surpassed by the plethora of affordable lunch options at its sidewalk cafés. See page 51.

Exploring the Toronto Islands by bike. A short and scenic ferry ride across Lake Ontario lies this bucolic chain of car-free islands. Stroll or cycle through its wooded landscapes – and enjoy a picnic on one of the islands' several beaches. See page 55.

Admiring exquisite paintings. Toronto's Art Gallery of Ontario boasts a wonderful collection of fine art and should not be missed. Prefer natural history? Head to the Royal Ontario Museum (see page 30) for dinosaurs, meteorites, and lots of bats. See page 49.

Listening to live music at the Drake Underground. This subterranean music venue is hot and appeals to music fans of all kinds. Catch local up-and-coming acts or see big-name performers here, and expect every night to be packed with locals and visitors alike. See page 117.

Hear the roar and feel the spray of Niagara Falls. Not far from Toronto, these world-famous waterfalls are a wonder to behold. View it early in the morning to avoid the crowds. See page 67.

Exploring the capital. Ottawa's imposing Parliamentary buildings steal the show, but the capital has much more, notably the stunning art of the National Gallery of Canada. See page 78.

Cruising Georgian Bay. Take a cruise on Georgian Bay, whose blue-black waters are confettied with rocky islets and their wispy pines. The scenery is wonderful – and there's chance to go wilderness hiking, too. See page 90.

By the end of the nineteenth century, **Toronto** had become a major manufacturing centre dominated by a conservative mercantile elite, which was loyal to the British interest and maintained a strong Protestant tradition. These same Protestants were enthusiastic about public education, just like the Methodist-leaning middle classes, who spearheaded social reform movements, principally Suffrage and Temperance. The trappings, however, remained far from alluring – well into the twentieth century Sunday was preserved as a "day of rest" and Eaton's store drew its curtains to prevent Sabbath window-shopping. Indeed, for all its capital status, the city was strikingly provincial by comparison with Montréal until well into the 1950s, when the opening of the St Lawrence Seaway gave the place something of a jolt and the first wave of immigrants began to transform the city's diversity.

In the 1960s, the economy exploded, and the city's appearance was transformed by the construction of a series of mighty, modernistic skyscrapers. This helter-skelter development was further boosted by the troubles in Québec, where the clamour for fair treatment by the Francophones prompted many of Montréal's Anglophone-dominated financial institutions and big businesses to up sticks and transfer to Toronto. Much to the glee of Torontonians, the census of 1976 showed that Toronto had become Canada's biggest city, edging Montréal by just one thousand inhabitants, and since then the gap has grown much wider. In the last forty years, Toronto's economy has followed the cycles of boom and retrenchment common to the rest of the country, though real estate speculation was especially frenzied in the 1980s and again in the early 2000s. Today, Toronto is a large and complex urban centre that continues to flourish, rich in culture and prosperous in its economy, retaining its proud heritage as an exciting, welcoming metropolis – but, at time of writing, fretful to emerge from the Covid-19 pandemic.

CLIMATE

Toronto and southwest Ontario enjoy a mild climate by Canadian standards, thanks to the regulating properties of Lake Ontario and Lake Erie; however,

Indigenous Ontario

This travel guide describes places that include the traditional lands and Treaty territories of many Indigenous Peoples, including the Algonquin and Huron-Wendat, and the Haudenosaunee Confederacy. Travelling offers us the privilege of being a guest among our hosts and building relationships with them. As you travel, take the opportunity to learn the history of a place; support Indigenous businesses and artists; and make connections with the people who continue to inhabit these lands.

A sunset view of the Toronto skyline from the Centre Island ferry

the climate gets harsher – and winters colder – the further north you go, with, for example, winters in Ottawa a good deal colder than Toronto. Most of the province experiences all four seasons distinctively with fall being a particularly good time to visit: it's then that the trees are ablaze in vivid reds, oranges, and yellows and there's little precipitation. Spring can be equally engaging, though the vagaries of the climate make it impossible to say precisely when winter will break. By comparison, summers, especially in Toronto and southwest Ontario, can be unbearably humid and hot, with temperatures reaching into the high 20s C (80s F).

POPULATION

With a population of just under three million, Toronto is the largest city in Canada and the fourth-largest in North America. Furthermore, the designated Greater Toronto Area (GTA), which includes the city's immediate suburbs, has a population of no less than 6 million. Of these 6 million residents, just under half were born outside of the country and today the influence of Toronto's 200-plus ethnicities is obvious in its cuisine, festivals, and dynamic neighbourhoods. From Koreatown, Chinatown, and Greektown, to Little Italy, Little Portugal, Little Jamaica, and Little India, the city pulsates with diversity: even the city's 911 emergency services are equipped to respond in over 150 unique languages.

LOCAL CUSTOMS

Toronto is a vibrant city, whose downtown core almost always feels safe and secure. Its inhabitants do not have a reputation for excessive friendliness, perhaps reserved is the best description, but – in the experience of this author at least – people are usually more than willing to offer advice and help. Eating and drinking are major pastimes in Toronto with most people having dinner reasonably early with drinking carrying on much later, sometimes into the wee hours. The same pattern emerges across the rest of Ontario, though most of the province's towns are much less ethnically diverse.

POLITICS AND ECONOMICS

Politically, Toronto and Ottawa tend to vote for the soft-left candidates of either the Liberal Party or the New Democratic Party, though local elections in Toronto rarely seem to gain much traction – only about 40 percent of the population actually vote. Out in the suburbs and the sticks, the population is generally more right wing with the Progressive Conservative Party of Ontario the dominant force. At the time of writing, Canada has a Liberal government and the Prime Minister is Justin Trudeau, who came to power in the federal election of 2015 and was re-elected, albeit by a much narrower margin, in 2019. The Progressive Conservative Party of

Pride Toronto is held every year in June

Ontario currently governs that province and has a substantial majority.

Economically, Ontario's timber and mining industries, massive hydroelectric schemes and myriad factories have kept the province at or near the top of the economic ladder for decades, its position bolstered by the emergence of Toronto as a major centre for finance, tech and tourism. Ontario's industrial success has also created massive environmental problem, to which some politicians are at least alert, perhaps no more so than in Toronto, where several proposed new developments trumpet their environmental credentials.

Toronto attracts most of the tourist headlines for Ontario as a whole and has long been a popular destination, not least for its welcoming sidewalk cafés, amazing ethnic restaurants, independent boutiques, top-ranking music venues and world-class museums. In 2020, the outbreak of Covid-19 laid the city low, but a rebirth and a revival approaches as the pandemic wanes.

TOP TIPS FOR VISITING TORONTO AND ONTARIO

Orientation in Toronto. Yonge Street is Toronto's principal north-south artery. Main drags perpendicular to Yonge use this intersection to change from west to east. Note, therefore, that 1000 Queen Street West is, for example, a long way from 1000 Queen Street East.

Public transport. Toronto has an excellent public transit system, an integrated network of subways, buses and streetcars. In addition, public bikes are available at docking stations around the city and can be borrowed for short to long periods via Bike Share Toronto (www.bikesharetoronto.com). Ottawa has a first-rate public transit system, too, and also offers a public bike scheme (www.bikeshare.com). Other than that, a limited network of trains and buses links the larger towns and cities of Ontario, but otherwise you will need your own transport; car hire is characteristically easy to arrange and not overly expensive.

Save time and money in Toronto. If you are intending to visit several major attractions in Toronto, then the CityPASS can save you money and, in some cases, enable you to bypass ticket lines. Further details on www.citypass.com.

Festivals. Every large town in Ontario has at least one major festival, but Toronto and Ottawa have several dozen each, celebrating everything from film and music through to food, lifestyle and sports. To see what's happening and when in Toronto, check out www.toronto.ca; in Ottawa, it's www.ottawafestivals.ca.

Sales tax and tipping etiquette. Expect a 13 percent sales tax on most retail purchases, plus an additional four percent tax on accommodation. When tipping for a service such as at a restaurant, plan on 15 to 20 percent if the service was more than satisfactory.

St Lawrence Market sells a variety of fresh produce

FOOD AND DRINK

Toronto's multicultural residents have brought wonderful diversity to the city's food scene. From authentic Chilean empanadas to Singaporean rice noodle soup, the variety of cuisines is seemingly endless, with a bit of everything for every palate.

Top chefs from all over the world are drawn to Toronto's ever evolving and eclectic food scene, with new restaurants popping up weekly. Locally sourced, natural ingredients, including meats and fresh produce, are key to most of the menus presented in the city, and a wide range of prices will suit all budgets.

LOCAL CUISINE

Besides the gravy-and-cheese-curds-covered fries dish called poutine, and the occasional maple syrup-infused offering, Canadian cuisine doesn't have a typical style that can easily be pinpointed. This is probably due to Canada, and especially Toronto, being home to such a diverse group of residents, many of whom have brought their cuisines with them.

On any given day in Toronto, hungry patrons are treated to a choice of meals that can include anything from a Cuban sandwich served out of a food truck Downtown, to a Korean rice bowl from an eatery in Koreatown, to the finest Portuguese seafood stew in Little Portugal. Italian pizzas, Japanese sushi, and Mexican tacos are all accounted for too, as are American-style steaks, Chinese dim sum, Indian curries, and Greek lamb dishes.

Although the range of flavours is wide, the communal ethos in Toronto's food scene is to use the freshest ingredients possible, many of which are sourced within a few hundred kilometres from the city. Sustainable and organic seafood, meats, and produce are of great importance to Toronto chefs in creating a menu, as is creativity, and a sense of adventure.

Of course, the typical burger, sandwich or pasta dish is widely available, and vegetarians and vegans will have no problem finding something that suits their dietary needs. Gluten and dairy-free options are often offered as well, as are smaller sized kids' meals.

Brunch is a big deal throughout the country and it's no different in Toronto. Often available on weekends only, from the hours of about 10am until 2pm, this in-between breakfast and lunch meal is meant to be enjoyed slowly, ideally accompanied by good friends. Eggs Benedict is the most popular dish, after which the choice of breakfast foods mingled with lunch items is endless.

Desserts are certainly not an after-thought in Toronto – or for that matter in

Eggs Benedict brunch at The Senator

Ontario as a whole – and can be indulged at any time of day. From flaky French chocolate croissants and colourful macarons to still-hot-from-the-oven donuts, to artisanal ice cream and over-the-top decorated cupcakes, anyone's sweet tooth is well sated. Handcrafted chocolates and thick milkshakes are also big hits with Torontonians.

Drinks too, come in both classic and highly creative forms, from single-origin organic coffees (a real fad in both Toronto and Ottawa) to Asian bubble teas, herb-infused specialty cocktails, and locally brewed craft beers. With Canada's largest wine-growing region, the Niagara Peninsula, only a couple of hours away, local wine is showcased heavily in the city.

WHERE TO EAT

Whether you're an adventurous, multi-course fine diner or simply looking for a quick budget-friendly bite, Toronto's convenient food trucks, innovative bistros, and top-notch restaurants serve up everything from vegan-friendly organic avocado toast to the juiciest local steak on offer.

BUDGET

To start off, however, Toronto's iconic food item has got to be the peameal bacon sandwich from the Carousel Bakery (see page 39) in the St Lawrence Market. Simple but delicious, and a must try for any visitor, it consists of a soft white bun filled with mustard-topped, Toronto-invented cured bacon made from pork

Farmers' Markets

Supplementing an already exciting food scene, Toronto also hosts authentic farmers' markets throughout the city and here you'll have the opportunity to connect with local farmers and artisans, see locals shopping for their weekly groceries, and be entertained by live music and street performers. Food trucks and other vendors of prepared food feature, too, so breakfast, lunch, and even dinner will be taken care of.

David Pecaut Square Market; 55 John Street; June–Oct Thu 8am–2.30pm.
The Distillery Historic District Sunday Market; 55 Mill Street; June–Oct Sun noon–5pm.
Evergreen Brick Works Farmers' Market; 550 Bayview Avenue; year-round Sat 8am–1pm (9am–1pm in winter).
John Street Farmers' Market; 197 John Street; June–Oct, Wed 3.30–7pm.
The Junction Farmers' Market; 2960 Dundas Street West; spring–fall Sat 9am–1pm.
Nathan Phillips Square Farmers' Market; 100 Queen Street West; June–Oct Wed 8am–2pm.
St Lawrence Farmers' Market; 93 Front Street East; year-round Sat 5am–3pm.
Trinity Bellwoods Farmers' Market; 790 Queen Street West; May–Oct, Tue 3–7pm.

Shawn Adler, chef at Pow Wow Café

loin, which is rolled in cornmeal, making it perfectly crispy.

Many other delicious and budget-friendly eats can be found at the St Lawrence Market, including the Lobster Rolls or the Boston Blue Fish & Chips from Buster's Sea Cove (see page 114), the Polish pierogies from European Delight (see page 114), and, for dessert, the Portuguese custard tarts from Churrasco's (see page 114).

Food trucks are another great option for getting a cheap and cheerful meal, with a choice ranging from soups and sandwiches to tacos, rice platters, and grilled meats, and so much more. Food trucks tend to move around and are scattered throughout the city, but a few best bet locations are at the intersection of University Avenue and College Street, and the intersection of Church and Bloor streets. Or check out www.torontofood-trucks.ca for current and upcoming food truck locations.

The funky and multicultural neighbourhood of Kensington Market is practically overflowing with affordable places to eat, from Caribbean fare at Rasta Pasta (see page 54) through to Mexican tacos from Seven Lives (see page 54).

Koreatown and Chinatown offer some excellent, good-value dining options, including authentic bibimbap rice bowls and dim sum, respectively, as does The Annex neighbourhood with its plentiful sandwich shops and cheap pub fare due to the large student population.

For Canadiana on a budget, try the bagels from Schmaltz Appetizing (see page 61), or the frybread tacos from The Pow Wow Café (see page 110) at 213 Augusta Avenue, in Kensington Market.

MID-RANGE

Along with an often stellar choice of craft beer on tap, the big brew pubs in Toronto and other big cities are a great choice for a meal anytime of day. In Toronto, the Distillery Historic District is home to the ever popular and spacious Mill Street Brew Pub (see page 44), or head to the Bellwoods Brewery (see page 116), a local favourite with a lively covered patio. Ossington Avenue is not only a hotspot for pubs and bars, but it's also an area known for its busy eateries ranging from Asian fusion cuisine to classic French fare. The hip Junction district around Dundas Street West and

Icy Souvenirs

Local icewines, such as those from Inniskillin Wines, and dessert wines are prized possessions in Toronto and make excellent gifts to take back home. If you don't get a chance to purchase these or other wines from the actual wineries, there are lots of stores that sell them in the city. The LCBO (Liquor Control Board of Ontario, www.lcbo.com) retail stores, with at least five locations just within the downtown core, are a good bet.

Enjoy dim sum in Chinatown

Niagara icewine, Peller Estate Winery

Keele Street is home to a plethora of craft breweries, juice cars, organic food stores, bakeries, and vegan restaurants.

The plethora of world cuisines in Toronto restaurants – and to a lesser extent Ottawa – tend to be in the budget to mid-range prices. Neighbourhoods such as Little Italy are lined up with excellent pizzerias and trattorias, but visitors will discover some great Mexican, Chinese, Korean, and Caribbean options here as well. Likewise, Little Portugal is home to various Portuguese restaurants but also several Italian joints, Japanese sushi spots, and Chinese buffet places.

HIGH-END

Toronto's downtown core, notably the Financial District, is where the expense-account restaurants tend to congregate with steakhouses, fine French and Canadian food, and seafood-focused restaurants leading the gastronomic charge. Even burgers become high-end in this neighbourhood, rising to wallet-searing versions at $30.

Toronto's Little Italy offers top-ranking dining options, including La Palma (see page 113) and Bar Isabel (see page 111).

DRINKS

Craft beer is still having a serious moment across all the larger cities of Ontario and especially in Toronto, which currently has over 35 breweries, located all over town, many of them small-batch, micro breweries. One of the most popular in Toronto is the Bellwoods Brewery (see page 116). It produces barrel-aged craft beers ranging from pale ales to stouts. The award-winning Amsterdam BrewHouse (see page 34) – the city's oldest brewery from 1986 – is known for its flavoursome IPAs and smooth lagers.

For classy and creative cocktails, wander around Entertainment District Downtown for plenty of options, or head to BarChef (see page 116) on Queen Street West – the best for cocktails in the city.

Wine bars in Toronto take things seriously, and offer top wines from the nearby Niagara Peninsula region, in addition to Québecois and British Columbian wines, plus imported varieties. Wines to sample are the organic Tawse Winery Chardonnays, the Trius Winery blended reds, Inniskillin Wines icewine, and the Peller Estates Ice Cuvée.

Toronto has over a dozen dedicated whiskey bars. The CC Lounge & Whiskey Bar (see page 116) and The Caledonian (see page 116) have top tasting menus.

Food and Drink Prices

Price for a two-course meal for one including a glass of wine (or other beverage):

$$$$ = over $60
$$$ = $45–60
$$ = $20–45
$ = under $20

The Entertainment District

ENTERTAINMENT

Many of the towns dotted across Ontario offer bijou entertainments – Stratford (see page 97), for example, has a prestigious Shakespeare festival – but Toronto and to a lesser extent Ottawa are the centre of all things cultural and have the best nightlife.

Toronto's nightlife scene is as varied as its neighbourhoods, but its epicentre is the downtown Entertainment District, which is stuffed to the gills with pubs and cocktail bars. Further out of the centre, Ossington Avenue, just west of Downtown, is home to some of the city's favourite bars, including The Dakota Tavern (see page 117), a saloon-style hot-spot with a variety of nightly music acts. And then there is adjacent Dundas Street West, which also has its fair share of popular watering holes and music joints.

Make a point, too, of exploring Queen Street West, which is lined with lively bars, speakeasies, and gastropubs as well as some of the city's best live music venues – for example The Horseshoe Tavern (see page 117) and the Drake Underground, part of the uber-cool Drake Hotel (see page 117).

Tips

The legal drinking age in Ontario is 19.
Expect long line-ups at bars and clubs on Friday and Saturday nights anytime after 10pm.
While Toronto's liquor laws require bars to stop serving alcohol by 2am, many bars, clubs and eateries can still remain open until 3, 4, and even 5am.
LGBTQ nightlife centres around Church and Wellesley streets – aka The Gay Village – northeast of Downtown, and The Annex neighbourhood is where the majority of students find cheap drinks in dive bars or stay up dancing until 5am at the Coda nightclub (see page 119). And Koreatown (see page 61) is undoubtedly the best location for karaoke bars.

MUSIC AND BALLET

The capacious Four Seasons Centre for the Performing Arts (see page 120) in the heart of Toronto showcases performances by the excellent Canadian Opera Company, one of the largest producers of opera in North America. Productions range from classic Mozart and Beethoven, to cutting-edge modern pieces sung in English.

The National Ballet of Canada, the largest in the country and founded in 1951, also performs at the Four Season Centre. Traditional and contemporary works are part of the company's repertoire, performed both within Canada and abroad.

Bright lights at the Elgin and Winter Garden Theatres

To hear the first-class Toronto Symphony Orchestra or the Toronto Mendelssohn Choir, head to the Roy Thomson Hall. While Toronto's Royal Conservatory presents classical, jazz, world, and pop music artists at the multi-balcony Koerner Hall, the 1901 Mazzoleni Concert Hall and the Temerity Theatre.

In Ottawa, the National Arts Centre (www.nac-cna.ca) is the city's cultural focus, presenting concerts by its resident orchestra and opera and ballet and dance from visiting troupes.

JAZZ AND BLUES

Toronto and Ottawa are big on jazz and blues. One of the greatest jazz pianists, Montréal's Oscar Peterson, embraced the jazz scene in Toronto in the 1940s and it has been flourishing ever since. In Toronto, catch up-and-coming and established artists at The Reservoir Lounge (see page 119) and The Rex Hotel (see page 119), whilst in Ottawa visit the Rainbow Bistro (www.therainbow.ca). Look out for the Beaches International Jazz Festival (www.beachesjazz.com).

THEATRE

Until Covid-19 hit, Toronto had a flourishing live theatre scene, covering the gamut from the avant-garde to the popular/populist. The Elgin and Winter Garden Theatres (see page 29) and Royal Alexandra Theatre (www.mirvish.com) cater for most tastes, but for something more adventurous, try the Soulpepper Theatre Company (www.soulpepper.ca). In Ottawa, visit the National Arts Centre (www.nac-cna.ca) or the Great Canadian Theatre Company (www.gctc.ca).

Nights Out in Toronto

Various Toronto attractions feature a special evening of the week or month where, after hours, the music is turned up, drinks might be offered, and guests can experience something different from the normal day-to-day schedule of the particular venue.

Art Gallery of Ontario. On the first Thursday evening of every month, the AGO presents a late-night event featuring a sneak peek exhibit viewing, live music, talks, and drinks. Check the AGO website (www.ago.ca) for the most current schedule of events.

Casa Loma. Throughout the year, this historic folly hosts events that include live jazz, comedy acts, and even murder mystery-type evenings, either in the lush gardens or inside this peculiar mansion.

Gardiner Museum. Salon 21 at the Gardiner Museum is a series of musical evenings taking place once or twice a month. These are free events and often include food and drinks.

Royal Ontario Museum. ROM Friday Night Live events are held most Friday nights in May and June and include top DJs, artists, drinks and nibbles, plus the opportunity to explore the galleries.

Kayaking on one of Ontario's beautiful lakes

OUTDOOR ACTIVITIES

From swimming and ice-skating through to hiking and cycling, Ontario caters for every sort of outdoor activity, both amidst the relatively tamed scenery of the south and in the wild wilderness of the north.

Ontario boasts some of the country's finest hiking, its multitude of provincial parks catering for every ability, from the easiest of lakeside strolls through to treks through rugged forested terrain. There is opportunity for long-distance canoeing too, with Algonquin Park being a choice destination. For something less energetic, Toronto offers a wide range of professional spectator sports, though here also there are lots of interesting walks, ravine hiking trails, and peaceful cycling routes.

WATERSPORTS

In Toronto, Lake Ontario may be the obvious place to head for if you're after some swimming, but frankly it's not ideal: the lake remains icy cold throughout the year and pollution levels can spike quickly, particularly near the city centre. More positively, kayaks, canoes, and paddleboards can be rented from the Harbourfront Canoe & Kayak Centre to explore Lake Ontario's hidden lagoons (www.paddletoronto.com) plus Toronto has a platoon of both outdoor and indoor swimming pools (www.toronto.ca). As for Ontario in general, there are literally thousands of lakes spread across

the province and many are perfect for a swim and/or canoe, though those around Georgian Bay are particularly recommended – and particularly beautiful.

BEACHES

Perhaps surprisingly, beachlife is one of Toronto's favourite summer pastimes, and locals flock to the nearby beaches to soak up some sun. Centre Island Beach, Gibraltar Point Beach, Ward's Island Beach, and Hanlan's Point Beach (a clothing-optional one), are some of the best beaches and are all located on the Toronto Islands, just a short ferry ride away.

Cherry Beach, just east of the Toronto Islands at the south end of Cherry Street, doesn't require a ferry ride and is perfect for watching windsurfers at play. The Beaches neighbourhood, east of Downtown, has, of course, plenty of lovely beaches, including Kew-Balmy Beach, which features a good concession stand.

ICE-SKATING

During the winter months, Canadians love to go ice-skating. All the larger settlements have outdoor, artificial ice-skating

Ice-skating in Nathan Phillips Square

rinks – Toronto has over 50 – and skate rental is commonplace, too. In Toronto, Nathan Phillips Square in front of City Hall is particularly popular, as is the rink at the Harbourfront Centre down on the lakeshore. In Ottawa, a particular delight is skating on the canals right in the centre of the city when they freeze over – as they usually do.

GOLF

Golf is a popular sport in southern Ontario and there are scores of courses to choose from – indeed the Greater Toronto Area (GTA) has over 200 of them. Try the legendary 18-hole Don Valley Golf Course in North York (www.donvalleyproshop.com), known for its beautiful natural setting, or have a go at the dramatic, Jack Nicklaus-designed Glen Abbey Golf Club in Oakville (www.glenabbey.clublink.ca).

HOCKEY

For many Canadians, hockey is more of a religion than a hobby, its main teams and players followed with supreme zeal. The acme of the professional sport is North America's National Hockey League (NHL; www.nhl.com) with thirty-one teams, seven of them in Canada, including the Ottawa Senators and the Toronto Maple Leafs. You can watch games in sports bars across the province or attend a game in person from October to April. Toronto's Hockey Hall of Fame (see page 38) is well worth a visit for sports fans, too.

BASKETBALL AND BASEBALL

North America's professional National Basketball Association (NBA; www.nbl) has one team hereabouts – the Toronto Raptors (www.nba.com/raptors), who should return to the Scotiabank Arena once Covid-19 restrictions are lifted. Canada's Major League Baseball (MLB) team, the Toronto Blue Jays (www.mlb.com/bluejays), plays at the Rogers Centre, though there are controversial plans afoot to have this demolished.

CANADIAN FOOTBALL

Arguably faster paced and more exciting than American football, Canada's own version of the game is the country's second most popular sport organized under the aegis of the Canadian Football League (www.cfl.ca). As for local, professional teams, Toronto has the Argonauts and Ottawa has the Redblacks, with the former having the larger following.

Toronto Stadiums

BMO Field: 170 Princes' Boulevard; tel: 416-815-5400; www.bmofield.com
Lamport Stadium: 1155 King Street West; tel: 416-392-1366; www.toronto.ca
Rogers Centre: 1 Blue Jays Way; tel: 416-341-1000
Scotiabank Arena (formerly the Air Canada Centre): 40 Bay Street; tel: 416-815-5500; www.scotiabankarena.com

BEST ROUTES

Dangerous Lagoon at Ripley's Aquarium of Canada

TORONTO CITY HIGHLIGHTS

If time is short, this day-long tour should suit visitors very well, picking out Toronto's most distinctive attractions, from the obvious – the CN Tower and the Royal Ontario Museum – to the more unusual, most memorably the Gardiner Museum of ceramic art and the double-decker Elgin and Winter Garden Theatres.

> **DISTANCE:** 7km (4.3 miles) walking and subway
> **TIME:** Full day
> **START:** Union Station
> **END:** Richmond Station
> **POINTS TO NOTE:** Check to see if the the Royal Ontario Museum (ROM) has discounted admission rates at certain hours and free guided tours before you set out – and the same applies to the Gardiner. Also to save money, the CN Tower, Ripley's Aquarium of Canada and the ROM are all part of the CityPASS scheme (see page 15).

Toronto has endless attractions, but this tour compresses a few of the best into one day, giving visitors a memorable time in the city and a taste for more.

CN TOWER

From the grand columned charms of **Union Station ❶**, dating from the 1920s, proceed west along Front Street to John Street, where you turn left to fol-low the signs to the **CN Tower ❷** – it's impossible to miss. The perspective from the top of the tower is dizzying, and if it's a clear day, you may just be able to make out Niagara Falls which is 127km away.

Over 2 million visitors a year head to the top of this famous tower, so expect a fair wait to get up there. One way to avoid the line-up is to go early in the morning, another is to head up after dark and admire it all lit up. A third option is to make a reservation at the tower's **360 The Restaurant**, skipping the line that way and enjoying a slow, rotating view of the whole city and surroundings while dining on fine Canadian cuisine. Visitors looking for more than just a view though should book an **EdgeWalk** experience (see page 37).

RIPLEY'S AQUARIUM OF CANADA

Right next door to the CN Tower is **Ripley's Aquarium of Canada ❸** (tel: 647-351-3474; www.ripleyaquariums.com/canada; times vary), an entertaining and interesting stop, with over 16,000 marine and freshwater specimens from

Inside the Elgin theatre

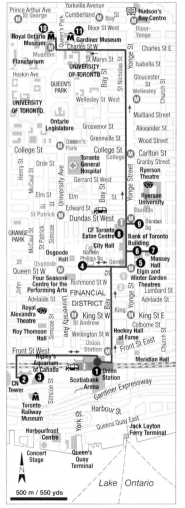

more than 450 species. Sharks, sea turtles, stingray, jellyfish and much more are on display here with plenty of hands-on activities that the kids will enjoy.

NATHAN PHILLIPS SQUARE

Backtrack to Union Station, either via the way you came or via the clearly signed PATH SkyWalk, and hop on Subway line 1 (Finch direction), heading north before getting out at Queen Station. From here, walk west along Queen Street West to **Nathan Phillips Square ❹**, a lively gathering place year round, especially in winter when the water feature turns into an ice-skating rink. The square is framed by both **new City Hall** (see page 40), a modernist structure dating from 1965, and the grand stonework of the **old City Hall** (see page 42), built in 1889. Both are worth examining for their admirable and distinctly different architectural styles. In front of the former is a large and distinctive sculpture *The Archer*, by Henry Moore, which stands as a proud beacon to the city's brave acceptance of modern art back in the 1960s.

ELGIN AND WINTER GARDEN THEATRES

Doubling back from Nathan Phillips Square along Queen Street West, the east side of Yonge Street boasts a cluster of well-preserved historical buildings, most notably the **Elgin and Winter Garden Theatres ❺** (tel: 416-314-3718;

Royal Ontario Museum

www.heritagetrust.on.ca; guided tours by appointment; charge for tours), at 189 Yonge Street – built in 1913 and the last surviving set of Edwardian double-decker theatres in the world. The Elgin, an old vaudeville theatre, is on the lower level, whilst up above is the Winter Garden, also a theatre but one that was sealed off for decades, its original decor left intact. Next door is the old **Bank of Toronto building** ❻, from 1905, and closeby is a long-time favourite music venue, **Massey Hall** ❼, which dates back to 1892.

CF TORONTO EATON CENTRE

Across the street from the Elgin and Winter Garden Theatres stretches the **CF Toronto Eaton Centre** ❽ (tel: 416-598-8560; www.cfshops.com; daily, hours vary), one of North America's busiest shopping malls, covering two city blocks and holding over 250 stores, restaurants, and assorted services spread across four flours. Several department stores, top global clothing brands and home decor stores will keep shoppers busy.

Modelled after a galleria in Milan, the vaulted glass ceiling gives an airy feel to this vast indoor space. Canadian artist Michael Snow created the flock of fibreglass Canada geese sculpture, called *Flight Stop*, that is suspended from the ceiling. Amongst a multitude of eating options, probably the pick is the **Saks Food Hall**, see ❶, located in the bottom level of the Saks Fifth Avenue department store.

DUNDAS SQUARE

If you emerge from the CF Toronto Eaton Centre at its northeast entrance, you'll be a few metres from **Dundas Square** ❾, long a popular meeting point and now a bland modern piazza illuminated by billboard screens and corporate logos, similar in style to New York City's Times Square. Dundas Square is often used as a site for festivals and art installations.

THE ROYAL ONTARIO MUSEUM (ROM)

Stroll north along Yonge Street for about 12 blocks, skirting the edge of the Gay Village, whose centre is generally reckoned to be at Church and Wellesley streets, before turning west onto Charles Street, altogether a 20-minute walk (or 5-minute subway ride). Thereafter, you'll soon spy the original stone facade of the **Royal Ontario Museum (ROM)** ❿ (tel: 416-586-8000; www.rom.on.ca; daily 10am– 5.30pm). Its striking, ultra-modern extension seems to tumble down onto Bloor Street West.

One of Toronto's most visited attractions, the ROM is the largest museum in Canada, featuring everything from exhibits on art and culture through to natural history and science. Over 6 million artifacts make up its fascinating collection, with notable specialisms in dinosaur fossils, African art, Egyptian treasures, and Art Deco objects, all showcased in more than 40 gallery and exhibition spaces.

Gardiner Museum workshop   *CF Toronto Eaton Centre*

Budding astronauts may find the meteorite collection in the Earth and Space galleries fascinating, as the ROM is home to the world's largest piece of Springwater pallasite – a rare meteorite discovered in 1931 near Springwater, Saskatchewan, that's 4.5 billion years old and weighs nearly 53kg (117lbs).

As part of the Natural History galleries, the simulated Bat Cave is entertaining for the whole family, featuring over 800 wax models of bats in a re-created habitat. Or view extinct species such as the dodo bird or the passenger pigeon, whose demise was especially poignant.

For a greater understanding of Canadian history, the Canadiana exhibit showcases fine Indigenous artifacts including wooden canoes, leather clothing, and weaponry. There's a display of works by Paul Kane (1810–71), an Irish-born Canadian painter whose famous paintings and sketches of the Indigenous were a resource for ethnologists and are often still used to this day for research.

GARDINER MUSEUM

At 111 Queen's Park sits Canada's outstanding national ceramics museum, the **Gardiner Museum ⓫** (tel: 416-586-8080; www.gardinermuseum.on.ca; daily 10am–5pm, till 9pm Fri). This holds a collection of over 4,000 pieces, ranging from earthenware vessels and sculptures from the Americas dating back to 3500 BC, to 16th-century English delftware and modern Canadian pottery. The museum offers clay workshops for all ages, and the gift shop is excellent for souvenirs; guided tours are often included with admission.

To end the day, hop onto Subway line 1 at the Museum Station and get off at Queen Station. Walk south on Yonge Street and west on Richmond Street West to one of the city's top restaurants, **Richmond Station**, see ❷.

Food and Drink

❶ SAKS FOOD HALL

Saks Fifth Avenue, 176 Yonge St; tel: 416-365-3130; www.pusateris.com; daily B, L, and D; $

More like a gourmet specialty food store, this is a collection of aisles and mini-restaurants featuring a well-curated assortment of the finest produce, baked goods, sweets, deli meats and cheeses, pantry items, exotic imports and prepared dishes. There's a Champagne bar, a yogurt bar, a juice bar and an Italian pizzeria, just to name a few options.

❷ RICHMOND STATION

1 Richmond Street West; tel: 647-748-1444; www.richmondstation.ca; Mon–Sat L and D; $$$

Seasonal, local, and creative Canadian dishes in a casual atmosphere. The Station Burger is a best seller, but the Duck Two Ways with a parsnip puree or the Rabbit Three Ways with braised bacon and onions are outstanding as well.

Strolling on the boardwalk

TORONTO'S HARBOURFRONT AND FORT YORK

Of all the neighbourhoods in Toronto, it is perhaps the Harbourfront which most encapsulates the burgeoning charms of the modern city – the area is readily explored along an appealing boardwalk. Near here too is a prime historical site – Fort York.

DISTANCE: 3km (2 miles) walking and partly by streetcar
TIME: Full day
START: Harbourfront Centre
END: Fort York National Historic Site
POINTS TO NOTE: This route begins with a walking tour of the Harbourfront Centre, which is readily reached via the 509 or 510 streetcars from Union Station. Alternatively, it's a 15-minute walk south along York Street from Union Station to the same starting point.

Right up until the 1980s, Toronto's lakeshore waterfront was a neglected sprawl, its old industrial buildings, reflecting its heyday as a major river port, left to rot and decay. Since then, the whole area has witnessed a spectacular transformation with many of its old buildings cleverly re-imagined, whilst other new structures have brought vim and vitality – as well as some of the priciest condos in the city. The focus is the **Harbourfront Centre**, a large, lakeshore leisure complex

with lashings of art and theatre that has become a popular target for both tourists and locals alike.

The main part of this walking route provides an easy introduction to this delightful waterfront zone and also includes a visit to the immaculately maintained British colonial stockade of **Fort York**. It's worth nothing that the Harbourfront Centre is a hop, skip and a jump from the passenger ferry terminal over to the Toronto Islands (see page 55).

HARBOURFRONT CENTRE

Nestled along the shores of Lake Ontario, the **Harbourfront Centre** ❶ (tel: 416-973-4000; daily 10am–11pm) is a 4-hectare (10-acre) waterfront park that was revitalized in the 1980s out of old and dishevelled warehouses – and is currently undergoing another spruce-up with the opening of new public spaces, Canada and Ontario Squares, as well as Exhibition Common, where the emphasis will be on food and market stalls. Pandemic lockdowns

The Power Plant

apart, the Harbourfront Centre buzzes all year around with events such as free festivals, big-name concerts, live performances, art installations and movie screenings.

Theatres, art galleries, cafés, stores, and design studios have a home here in the spacious buildings. The Bill Boyle Artport inside the Harbourfront Centre's main building was transformed from an old trucking garage into an art gallery on the first level. The Artport Gallery, specifically, features ongoing exhibitions of local and global contemporary design, craft, photography, and architecture.

QUEEN'S QUAY TERMINAL

On the eastern side of the Harbourfront Centre is the handsome, well-proportioned **Queen's Quay Terminal ❷**. Built in 1927, this Art Deco structure was originally an old warehouse and cold store, but it has been converted into condominiums with a smart shopping mall complex on the ground floor. It includes a Sobeys grocery store – a handy stop for picnic items – as well as a platoon of fast-food eateries.

Note that just 500 metres to the east of Queen's Quay Terminal is the Jack Layton Ferry Terminal, from where passenger ferries depart for the Toronto Islands (see page 55).

Take in the lake views as you stroll the boardwalk that runs from the Queen's Quay Terminal, admiring the cruise ships, yachts, and sailboats moored along the water's edge, and enjoy the street performers during the summer months. Inviting cafés and pubs with large waterside patios, tourist shops, ice cream vendors, and art galleries are all accessible along the boardwalk, plus plenty of shady spots to sit and relax.

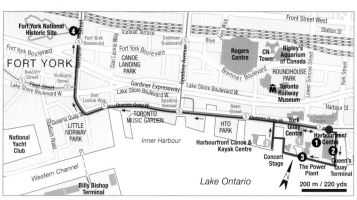

Amsterdam BrewHouse

For a refreshingly strong coffee accompanied by a freshly baked pastry, stop by the **Boxcar Social**, see ①, on the first level of the main Harbourfront Centre building, facing the lake. Or head back here later in the evening for a tasty sundowner out on the waterfront patio.

THE POWER PLANT

A recommended stop is **The Power Plant** ❸ (tel: 416-973-4949; www.the powerplant.org; Tue–Sun 10am–5pm, Thu until 8pm, holiday Mon; free), one of the city's most adventurous contemporary art galleries, occupying an imaginatively converted 1920s power station. It features regularly rotated exhibitions, often of emerging Canadian talent, which may be indecipherable to some, but are undoubtedly inspirational to others. They also show films and offer workshops for many of the creative arts – and are intertwined with the outstanding Toronto Writers' Collective. The gallery is located beside the main boardwalk and shares its power-station premises with the **Harbourfront Centre Theatre** (tel: 416-973-4000; www.harbourfrontcentre. com), which itself offers a wide-ranging programme of performing arts. The Power Plant also hosts educational programs and public events and publishes art books. There are free 30-minute guided tours of the gallery and weekly free lectures on revolving around the current exhibit.

AMSTERDAM BREWHOUSE

Next door to The Power Plant is the **Natrel Pond**, which doubles as an ice-skating rink during the winter months, free for all to use, with evening entertainment on the weekend by various DJs. Hockey is very much Canada's sport of choice, so don't be amazed at just how competent local toddlers are on their skates. Heading around the corner, passing by the Concert Stage, a dinky pedestrian bridge takes you to the **Amsterdam BrewHouse**, see ②. You can't reserve a spot on the patio so be prepared to wait during the warmer months, but it's well worth it. Sip a cold brew here or sample some delicious pub grub and make the most of the view before catching the streetcar on to Fort York.

FORT YORK NATIONAL HISTORIC SITE

From the Harbourfront Centre, take the 509 Harbourfront streetcar westbound to the stop at Fleet Street and Fort York Boulevard; from here, it's a signed, 5minute-walk north to the **Fort York National Historic Site** ❹ (tel: 416-392-6907; www.fortyork.ca; daily 10am–5pm), Toronto's leading historical attraction. Built on the shores of Lake Ontario in 1793, Fort York was designed to bolster British control of the Great Lakes. Since that time, landfill has slowly pushed the lakeshore south-

Fort York National Historic Site

wards and marooned the fort – which was attractively reconstructed in the 1930s – under the shadow of the (elevated) Gardiner Expressway.

At first, Fort York was a half-hearted, poorly fortified affair, partly because of a lack of funds, but mainly because it was too remote to command much attention – never mind that the township of York had become the capital of Upper Canada. However, in 1811, a deterioration in Anglo-American relations, that was soon to lead to war, put it on full alert. There was a sudden flurry of activity as the fort's ramparts and gun emplacements were strengthened, but it was still too weak to rebuff the American army that marched on York in 1813. After the war, Fort York, which the Americans occupied only briefly before abandoning it, was rebuilt and its garrison made a considerable contribution to the development of Toronto, as York was renamed in 1834. The British army moved out in 1870 and their Canadian replacements stayed for another sixty years; the fort was opened as a museum in 1934. Throughout the summer, costumed guides give the low-down on colonial life and free plans of the fort are issued at reception.

The fort's carefully restored earth and stone ramparts are low-lying, thick and constructed in a zigzag pattern, both to mitigate against enemy artillery and to provide complementary lines of fire. They enclose a haphazard sequence of stone and brick buildings, notably a couple of well-preserved blockhouses, complete with heavy timbers and snipers' loopholes. In one of them, an introductory video outlines the history of the fort and an exhibit explores the various military crises that affected colonial Canada. Other buildings well worth a close examination include the former Officers' Quarters and Mess, which has several period rooms and two original money vaults, hidden away in the cellar.

Food and Drink

① BOXCAR SOCIAL

235 Queens Quay West; tel: 647-349-1210; www.boxcarsocial.ca; daily; $$
Not just a pleasant, spacious café, this industrial-feel eatery with a lovely lakeview patio offers an Italian-inspired lunch and dinner menu with sandwiches, salads, and snacks to match its excellent and well-curated coffee, craft beer, whiskey and wine menus.

② AMSTERDAM BREWHOUSE

245 Queens Quay West; tel: 416-504-1020; www.amsterdambeer.com; daily; $
Spacious lakeside pub with a wide selection of draft, seasonal and cask offerings. Ask for a tasting flight to sample their beers, or go on a brief brewery tour. Try getting a seat outside on the patio facing the harbour, then pair your drinks with some freshly baked pretzels, their famous buffalo cauliflower appetizer and a juicy burger.

The CN Tower SkyPod

TORONTO – DOWNTOWN WEST

One of Toronto's top sights is the CN Tower, once the world's highest tower. Nearby are reminders of the city's earlier history, notably Union Station and the Anglican cathedral, not to mention its sporting obsessions at the Hockey Hall of Fame.

DISTANCE: 3.2km (2 miles) walking or partly by streetcar
TIME: Full day
START: CN Tower
END: Drake One Fifty
POINTS TO NOTE: The St Lawrence Market is always closed on Mondays and the food vendors are also closed on Sundays, so it may be best to do this tour on any other day as you won't want to miss all the tasty offerings inside. The Cathedral Church of St James is free to enter and has an 18-voice choir that sings at 11am and 4.30pm every Sunday. Pipe organ recitals are at 1pm on Tuesdays and 4pm on Sundays.

Sandwiched between Queen Street West to the north, Front Street West to the south, Yonge Street to the east, and Spadina Avenue to the west, the Downtown West neighbourhood contains not only stacks of glimmering glass condos, but also the city's entertainment, fashion, and financial districts. It's where Torontonians work, play, and sleep. In this route we've also included the city's mascot, the CN Tower, just south of Front Street, and the atmospheric St Lawrence Market, just to the east.

This route starts at the CN Tower; the closest subway station is Union Station, from where it's a short walk southwest along the clearly signposted walkway.

CN TOWER

Wherever you may be in the city, the slender concrete structure of the **CN Tower** ❶ (tel: 416-868-6937; www.cntower.ca; daily 8.30am–11pm) is nearly always visible. Built in 1976 by the Canadian National Railway Company (CN), its original purpose was to act as a TV and radio communication platform for the city, and as a status symbol reflecting CN's ambitions.

The viewpoint from the 447-metre (1,465ft) interior SkyPod (equivalent to 147 building stories) has, of course, an even more stunning vantage point. The Observation Deck also boasts a glass floor for those who aren't scared of looking straight down.

Union Station

For an even more thrilling view, literally, book an EdgeWalk experience – the world's highest full circle hands-free walk on a 1.5m (5ft) wide ledge encircling the top of the tower's main pod, 356m (1,168ft) high. Attached to a harness linked to an overhead safety rail you can literally let yourself hang, suspended over the city. Wow!

With views of up to 160km (100 miles), reaching as far away as Niagara Falls and New York State, standing at any of the elevated levels of the tower will offer a spectacular experience. This famous Toronto structure is certainly the number one tourist attraction of the city, with over 1.5 million visitors reaching the top levels every year.

To avoid the queues, try to arrive before 11am or after 6pm or consider dining at the tower restaurant, **360 The Restaurant**, see ➊. Admission is included with your meal.

FRONT STREET

Exiting east from the CN Tower via the PATH SkyWalk, head toward Union Station, whose imposing neoclassical columns face out onto Front Street West.

Union Station is a distinguished Beaux Arts structure that was designed in 1907 and completed twenty years later. The highlight is the vast main hall, which boasts a coffered and tiled ceiling of graceful design and with the flavour of a medieval cathedral – muffled sounds echo through its stone cloisters.

Directly across Front Street is the opulent **Fairmont Royal York**, which was the tallest and largest building in the British Empire when it opened in 1929. The architects here opted for a Beaux Arts style to match Union Station, but in lieu of the formal symmetries of the station, they gave the hotel an irregular cascading facade reminiscent of a French château.

Along Front Street West, another Beaux-Arts style building on the south side of the street is now visible. This is the **Dominion Public Building**, built in 1926 and now housing office space for the Canada Revenue Agency.

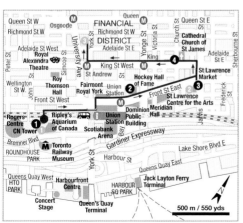

Hockey Hall of Fame, a tribute to Canada's national obsession

HOCKEY HALL OF FAME

At the intersection of Yonge Street and Front Street West is the **Hockey Hall of Fame ❷** (tel: 416-360-7765; www.hhof.com; Mon–Sat 9.30am–6pm, Sun 10am–6pm), a sports museum dedicated to the history of ice hockey. Inside, visitors can see the Stanley Cup, hockey's Holy Grail and shoot real pucks, among other interactive games. Not surprisingly, perhaps, the NHL team with the most player inductees honoured at the Hockey Hall of Fame is the Toronto Maple Leafs, with 64 out of a total of 276 players.

The museum is housed in an impressive former Bank of Montreal head office building from 1885. The ornate facade with intricate carvings, columns and pediments was meant to evoke a prosperous and secure image of the bank.

Continuing east on Front Street, passing by the **Meridian Hall** and the **St Lawrence Centre for the Arts**, the back of the 1892 flatiron **Gooderham Building** can be seen after Berczy Park. The large mural is by Canadian artist Derek Michael Besant, using a trompe l'oeil effect.

ST LAWRENCE MARKET

From the Gooderham Building, it's one more block east along Front Street to the historic **St Lawrence Market ❸** (tel: 416-392-7219; www.stlawrencemarket.com; Tue–Sun 8am–6pm), a perfect spot for a break. Try the peameal bacon sandwich from the **Carousel Bakery**, see ❼.

The site of a public market since 1803, the St Lawrence Market is divided into three buildings – South, North, and the Hall. The main and lower levels of the South Market contain over 120 specialty food and craft vendors, with fresh and local produce, flowers, meats, seafood, baked goods, prepared foods, and more.

The **North Market** is primarily known for its Saturday Farmers' Market where producers from the surrounding area bring their seasonal goods. On Sundays, this space is filled with over 80 antiques

Browsing at the St Lawrence Sunday antiques market

dealers. The **St Lawrence Hall**, north, across the street on King Street East and built in 1850, is used as a venue for concerts, exhibitions and public events.

KING STREET

Stroll north up Jarvis Street after the St Lawrence Hall, to King Street East, where you can continue walking west along King Street or take streetcar 504 to York Street – and the end of this route. If you proceed along King Street, you'll spy the Anglican **Cathedral Church of St James** ❹ (tel: 416-364-7865; www.stjamescathedral.ca; Sun–Fri 7am–5.30pm, Sat 9am–5pm; free), whose yellowish stone is offset by copper-green roofs and a slender spire. A top example of the neo-Gothic style, the cathedral holds scores of pointed-arch windows and acres of sturdy buttressing. The highlight of the interior is the stained-glass windows.

Art galleries, spas, luxury home decor stores, cafés, restaurants and bars line King Street. As you continue west, the historical architecture makes way for modern office buildings and condominiums. There's plenty of choice for food. Our pick is the artsy **Drake One Fifty**, see ❸, with its creative Canadiana cuisine and busy streetside patio.

Food and Drink

❶ 360 THE RESTAURANT
301 Front Street West; tel: 416-362-5411; www.cntower.ca; daily; $$$
At 1,151 feet (351m), dining at this revolving restaurant at the top of the CN Tower is an unforgettable experience, and not just for the incredible views. 360 The Restaurant features a fine Canadian menu, with a seafood focus including Atlantic salmon, cod and lobster dishes. The first-rate wine list is all Canadian, too.

❷ CAROUSEL BAKERY
93 Front Street East (Upper Level); tel: 416-363-4247; www.stlawrencemarket.com; Tue–Fri 9am–5pm and Sat 5am–4pm; $
Home of the world-renowned Canadian peameal bacon sandwich, this Portuguese bakery has been visited by many celebrities and countless tourists and locals love it too. On a typical busy Saturday, an incredible 2,000 of their famous sandwiches will be sold. Cash only.

❸ DRAKE ONE FIFTY
150 York Street; tel: 416-363-6150; www.thedrake.ca; daily; $$$
An offshoot from the iconic Drake Hotel on Queen West Street, this big, colourful brasserie is art-adorned and features lovely vintage and modern decor – just like the hotel. The menu is new Canadian, so you can expect a bit of everything – salads, tapas, pizzas, seafood, and burgers, though all refined and upscale. Cocktails, too, are chic and delicious.

TORONTO'S HISTORIC HEART

Toronto's two city halls – one new, one old – illustrate the transformation of the city into a major modern metropolis, whilst its industrial heritage is recalled in style amongst the galleries and bistros of the Distillery District.

DISTANCE: 3km (1.9 miles) walking or partly by streetcar
TIME: Full day
START: Toronto City Hall
END: Distillery Historic District
POINTS TO NOTE: A free brochure detailing a self-guided tour of the new City Hall is available from the information desk inside, or it can be downloaded online (www.toronto.ca). During the winter months, the reflecting pool in the Nathan Phillips Square is used as a skating rink, which is open to the public and free.

Starting at the heart of the city, this tour gives a brief history lesson of Toronto spanning over a century. In addition, there are plenty of side detours, if time permits. If you are starting this tour in the morning, and you haven't had breakfast yet, then the international chain **Eggspecta-tion**, see ①, is just what you're looking for before you set out on a full day of walking around the city.

TORONTO CITY HALL

As you stand in **Nathan Phillips Square**, with the striking modernist **Toronto City Hall** ① (tel: 416-397-5000; www.toronto.ca; Mon–Fri 8.30am–4.30pm; free) in the centre and proud municipal buildings all around, the sense of this being the heart of the city is clear. Thousands of visitors come to this engaging space on a daily basis and it's the ideal start to this walking route.

Chosen from an international competition consisting of more than 500 competitors from 42 countries, it was won by Finnish architect Viljo Revell. The new Toronto City Hall was opened in 1965 and immediately became the unique civic symbol that it is to this day.

Just inside the entrance, local artist David Partridge created the mesmerizing sculptural mural *Metropolis* out of more than 100,000 copper and galvanized nails.

The large bronze sculpture in front, *Three-Way Piece No. 2*, but more commonly known as *The Archer*, was cre-

Nathan Phillips Square

ated by British artist Henry Moore in 1965. It was commissioned to follow the flowing lines of the new city hall structure, and it was a highly controversial piece at that time, considering the cost ($100,000CAD) and its unconventional, abstract shape.

Less than a decade later, this purchase encouraged Moore to bestow hundreds of pieces of his work – sculptures, prints and drawings – to the Art Gallery of Ontario, AGO, (see page 49), which now houses the largest public collection of his art in the entire world.

From the air, the **new City Hall** resembles a giant unblinking eye, earning the nickname 'The Eye of the Government'. The futuristic concrete structure was built to replace the Old City Hall, the copper-topped Romanesque-style building with the distinctive clock tower across the street.

PODIUM GREEN ROOF

Atop City Hall lies a hidden sanctuary: just follow the winding ceremonial ramp that leads from the Nathan Phillips Square to the **Podium Green Roof** (www.toronto.ca) consisting of environmentally-conscious landscaped gardens, and it's open to the public year-round. Wooden benches are scattered around, while a concrete path runs throughout it. Plants are arranged according to colour, ranging from yellows and oranges in the west,

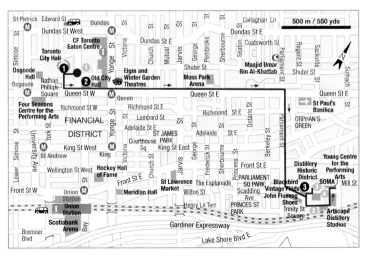

Toronto's modernist City Hall

to purples and reds in the east. At night, it's the LED lights that give the gardens flashes of colour.

OLD CITY HALL

Designed a National Historic Site, the **Old City Hall ❷** (tel: 416-338-0338; www.toronto.ca; Mon–Fri 8am–6.30pm; free) is a flamboyant pseudo-Romanesque structure completed in 1889 to a design by Edward J. Lennox, who was also responsible for the city's famous faux castle, Casa Loma (see page 59).

The sandstone exterior features a 103-metre (340ft) clock tower with four bronze gargoyles near the top, though these gargoyles are replicas as the originals have been lost. Near the building's entrance, several faces are carved in the stone pillars, faces – more accurately caricatures – of the leading political figures of the day with whom Lennox had a fractious relationship: they quarrelled over the soaring construction costs.

Inside, original features of the Old City Hall include an impressive staircase, an arcade with murals of early pioneers and angels, intricate stained-glass windows, marble columns, and a mosaic floor. Today, the Old City Hall is used as a courthouse but the building is open to the public during regular business hours. Future plans, among several, are to turn the building into a museum.

Across Bay Street from both city halls is the sprawling **CF Toronto Eaton Centre** shopping complex. If the weather is inclement, or you simply feel like some retail therapy, this is the place to go. The food court is decent here as well, if you're feeling peckish at all.

Beyond the CF Toronto Eaton Centre, on the opposite side of Yonge Street are the Elgin and Winter Garden Theatres, the Bank of Toronto building, and around the corner on Shuter Street, the Massey Hall – these are all appealing heritage buildings that are certainly worth a look, even if it is just from the outside.

DISTILLERY HISTORIC DISTRICT

From the Old City Hall, walk east along Queen Street for approximately 10 blocks, taking breaks in the parks along the way if you desire, or take the 501 streetcar eastbound, getting off at Parliament Street. Walk south along Parliament Street, heading into the **Distillery Historic District ❸** (tel: 416-364-1177; www.thedistillery district.com; Mon–Wed 10am–7pm, Thu–Sat 10am–8pm, Sun 11am–6pm; free), starting at Gristmill Lane, which is located in between Parliament and Mill Street. A slightly more convenient alternative route is to walk three blocks south from Queen Street all the way to King Street. After that you can then hop on the 504 street-

Old City Hall clock

car, which travels east to the Distillery District.

A National Historic Site, the whole Victorian-era and fully restored 5-hectare (13-acre) site features around 50 brick and stone heritage buildings. They date back to as early as 1859, all originally belonging to the Gooderham & Worts Distillery complex. This was once the world's largest distillery, which began with a simple sill in 1837.

Being car-free, pedestrians can wander along the cobblestone streets here and peak into the art galleries, design studios and chic clothing boutiques housed in high-ceiling, converted warehouses and 21st century modern buildings, at their leisure. Whimsical sculptures are sprinkled throughout the streets, many allowing for perfect photo opportunities, so make sure that you bring your camera along with you, too.

For those who are looking to go shopping, head to **Bergo Designs**, at 28 Tank House Lane, with its selection of award-winning, stylish home decor, unusual watches and fun Canadiana items. Or, alternatively, try **Blackbird Vintage Finds**, at 11 Trinity Street, for a treasure trove of anything from new French soaps to antique American typewriters.

GRISTMILL LANE

As brick-lined **Gristmill Lane** narrows, a **John Fluevog Shoes** store is visible on the right. A Vancouver original dating from the early 1970s, this quirky shoe store sells unique eye candy for both women and men's feet in quality leather and outlandish designs. Gristmill Lane opens up to Trinity Street, which is adorned by larger-than-life public art and is definitly worth an explore.

TRINITY STREET

Trinity Street is home to the main public square and is where outdoor markets, festivals and other events are frequently held. For a relaxing coffee break, grab a seat either outside or inside the cozy, atmospheric **Balzac's**, see ❷. For a more substantial but still casual lunch, try the **Brick Street Bakery**, see ❸.

CASE GOODS LANE AND TANK HOUSE LANE

The Case Goods Warehouse and the Cannery Building, just east of the Trinity Street square, is home to dozens of artists' studios, known collectively as the **Artscape Distillery Studios**. Pop into one of the open studios for a glimpse – or even a purchase – of local artwork. It may just be the most memorable souvenir on your travels in Toronto.

Farther up, on Tank House Lane, is **SOMA** – an exquisite chocolatier located in a former whisky-ageing

The atmospheric Distillery District

tankhouse. Try their truffle chocolates, which come in unusual flavours such as strawberry rhubarb, brown butter, bergamot, douglas fir, magnolia peach and jasmine. SOMA uses all natural flavourings, locally grown fruit where possible, and both fair-trade and organic cacao beans.

If the thought of dinner sounds ideal by now, the **Mill Street Brew Pub**, see ④, is an easy choice for food, followed by an enjoyable theatrical performance at the **Young Centre for the Performing Arts** (tel: 416-866-8666; www.youngcentre.ca). The Young Centre features a wide range of high-quality live performances, from classic dramas to satires, fringe and comedies. Attending a show here is a great way to end your day of exploring.

Food and Drink

① EGGSPECTATION
Bell Trinity Square, 483 Bay Street; tel: 416-979-3447; www.eggspectation.ca; daily B and L; $
A Montréal original, this small but now international breakfast chain will start your day off just right. Begin with Belgian waffles topped with strawberries and a salted maple caramel sauce and eggs Benedict with sautéed Maritime lobster. Sit outside on the patio if you can get a seat, and watch busy Torontonians heading off to work.

② BALZAC'S
1 Trinity Street; tel: 416-207-1709; www.balzacs.com; daily B, L, and early D; $
Housed in an 1895 pump house, this two-storey Parisian-style café serves excellent organic coffees and accompanying snacks. Pick up a bag of the Atwood Blend freshly roasted coffee beans for a splendid souvenir.

③ BRICK STREET BAKERY
27 Trinity Street; tel: 416-214-4949; www.brickstreetbakery.com; daily B, L, and early D; $
Great little bakery with a few spots to sit inside and outside. The ultra-fresh sandwiches, pastries, and desserts are all made using organic flour, natural meats, and local vegetables. Try the Cornish Pasties and the Sausage Rolls for savoury, satisfying goodness, too.

④ MILL STREET BREW PUB
21 Tank House Lane; tel: 416-681-0338; www.millstreetbrewery.com; daily L and D, Sat–Sun B; $$
Spacious brewpub that produces an organic lager, refreshing ales and a tangy stout. The top-ranking pub food menu includes generous portions of various poutines, curries, and burgers. Daily tours of the onsite brewery are available, or sit out on the patio and enjoy people watching.

Fairmont Royal York Hotel

GRAND TORONTO: ALONG UNIVERSITY AVENUE

The most appealing of Toronto's main boulevards, University Avenue slices through the heart of the city, passing a platoon of its most interesting buildings – both historic, like the Fairmont Royal York Hotel, and the modern, notably the Bata Shoe Museum.

DISTANCE: 3.2km (2 miles) walking
TIME: Full day
START: *Triad*
END: Bata Shoe Museum
POINTS TO NOTE: Although this is meant as a walking route, there are five subway stations along the way if walking continuously is not feasible.

Standing outside of Union Station on Front Street West, University Avenue begins rather inauspiciously at a busy intersection, but persevere as things improve as you stroll north with the massive silhouette of the Ontario Legislative Assembly Building hoving into view soon enough.

TRIAD SCULPTURE

Get your bearings and start this route at the *Triad* ❶, a 10.5-metre (35ft) sculpture of three, twisting, stainless steel columns that stands on Front Street West at York – footsteps from the beginning of University Avenue. Designed by Canadian sculptor Ted Bieler in 1984, it was commissioned

to mark the occasion of Toronto's 150th birthday, symbolizing the growth of the city and the unity of its residents.

FAIRMONT ROYAL YORK HOTEL

Close to the *Triad* sculpture, on Front Street West, is the grand, copper-topped **Fairmont Royal York Hotel ❷**. Built in 1929 by the Canadian Pacific Railway, it was, at the time of its construction, a state-of-the-art delight, boasting 10 ornate elevators ascending to all 28 floors. Luxury upon luxury, each room had a private radio and en-suite bathroom. There was space for the Imperial Room, one of the city's legendary nightclubs from the 1940s till the 1990s, hosting famous entertainers including the likes of Marlene Dietrich, Peggy Lee, and Ella Fitzgerald.

TORONTO DOMINION GALLERY OF INUIT ART

Behind the Royal York Hotel, in the TD South Tower at 79 Wellington Street West, is the delightful **Toronto Domin-**

The Great Library at Osgoode Hall

ion Gallery of Inuit Art ❸ (tel: 416-982-8473; www.td.com; Mon–Fri 8am–6pm, Sat–Sun 10am–4pm). On display here are some 200 original soapstone, bone, antler, and ivory sculptures, in addition to prints and ceramics, all the work of Inuit artists from Canada's arctic, mostly dating from the 1940s–60s. The collec-

tion was founded in 1967 by the Toronto Dominion Bank to commemorate Canada's 100th birthday, a celebration of both the country's past and future via art.

Doubling back along Wellington Street, turn right to stroll north along University Avenue until, just beyond Adelaide Street West, you reach the **Momofuku Noodle Bar**, see ➊, an excellent spot for lunch or dinner (the latter requiring reservations), specializing in Asian-fusion noodle dishes.

FOUR SEASONS CENTRE FOR THE PERFORMING ARTS

Pushing on along University Avenue, it's the shortest of strolls to the **Four Seasons Centre for the Performing Arts ❹**, a large and modern glass structure that is home to the Canadian Opera Company and the National Ballet of Canada. The main glass facade has a computer-controlled exterior shade that responds to weather sensors, keeping the interior at comfortable temperatures, even on the hottest of days. The glass staircase inside the Isadore and Rosalie Sharp City Room is one of a kind – it's the longest free-spanning glass staircase in the world.

Major performances take place at the centre, from big-ticket productions to chamber pieces and large-scale orchestras. During the months of late September through May, this venue also hosts a Free Concert Series on most Tuesdays and Thursdays at noon.

Canada Life Building

OSGOODE HALL

Across Queen Street West from the Four Seasons is **Osgoode Hall ⑤**, a handsome neoclassical mansion surrounded by an ornate wrought-iron fence and leafy gardens. This landmark building dates from 1832 and originally served as the headquarters for the Law Society of Ontario. It now houses the Ontario Court of Appeal, and other branches of the court, which spill over into the modern, 1960s Toronto Courthouse next door.

The old courthouse, the Great Library, and the Convocation Hall can all be viewed via a self-guided tour or with a Law Society staff member during the summer months, usually starting at 1.15pm.

For a treat, lunch at the **Osgoode Hall Restaurant**, see ❶, located on the east side of the building, inside the Convocation Hall. The menu is farm-to-table, featuring locally grown produce and meats. There's a security check to enter the main building as it's an active courthouse.

CAMPBELL HOUSE MUSEUM

West across University Avenue from Osgoode Hall is the **Campbell House Museum ⑥** (tel: 416-597-0227; www.campbellhousemuseum.ca; Tue–Fri 9.30am–4.30pm, Sat–Sun noon–4.30pm), an elegant Georgian mansion dating from 1822. The one-time home of Sir William Campbell, Chief Justice and Speaker of the Legislative Assembly, the Hall continued to be the residence of prominent Torontonians until 1890, after which it was used by various companies as office space. The mansion's original location was actually 1.5km (1 mile) to the southeast of its current location on Adelaide Street; it was moved here in 1972 to make way for a parking lot. Today, the well-preserved interior is distinguished by its woodwork and circular stairway. Costumed guides preside.

CANADA LIFE BUILDING

Next door rises the monumental Beaux-Arts **Canada Life Building ⑦**. Constructed in 1931, it served as the headquarters for Canada Life, Canada's oldest, and at that time largest, insurance company. It still serves as office space. The building is best known for its Art Deco rooftop weather beacon, whose colour codes provide a four-times-daily local weather forecast. A steady green light equals clear conditions, steady red predicts overcast, flashing red equals rain, and flashing white means snow.

QUEEN'S PARK

Striding north along University Avenue, it takes 10 minutes to get to the southern tip of **Queen's Park ⑧**, whose lawns are dotted with statues of the great, the good and the not-so-good, including Queen Victoria, John Graves Simcoe and the Tory radical, William Lyon Mackenzie, who led a rebellion for greater democracy here in Canada in 1837.

The pink sandstone Ontario Legislative Assembly Building

ONTARIO LEGISLATIVE ASSEMBLY BUILDING

Queen's Park is overshadowed by the sandstone bulk of the **Ontario Legislative Assembly Building** ❾ (guided tours only; tel: 416-325-7500; www.ola.org), which was completed in the 1890s. The building could hardly be described as elegant, but its ponderous symmetries do have a certain appeal with block upon block of roughly dressed stone assembled in the full flourish of the Romanesque Revival style. The foyer leads to the thickly carpeted Grand Staircase, whose massive timbers are supported by gilded iron pillars. Beyond is the capacious Legislative Chamber, where the formality of the wooden panels is offset by a series of little whimsical carvings – look for the owl above the government benches and the hawk above those of the opposition.

BATA SHOE MUSEUM

Head west then north through the campus of the **University of Toronto**, whose stone colleges were built in the style of Oxford and Cambridge. After 15 minutes, you'll reach Bloor Street West, where the **Bata Shoe Museum** ❿ (tel: 416-979-7799; www.batashoemuseum.ca; Mon–Sat 10am–5pm, Sun noon–5pm), occupies a building designed to look like a shoe box, the roof set at an angle to suggest a lid resting on an open box. Funded by Sonja Bata of the Bata shoe manufacturing family, the museum holds a range of footwear, from pointed shoes from medieval Europe, where different social classes were allowed various lengths of toe to tiny Chinese silk shoes worn by women whose feet had been bound. You'll find a range of specialist footwear, such as French chestnut-crushing clogs from the nineteenth century; and celebrity footwear – Marilyn Monroe's stilettos, Princess Diana's red court shoes, and Elton John's bright platform shoes attract most attention.

Food and Drink

❶ MOMOFUKU NOODLE BAR

190 University Avenue; tel: 647-253-8000; www.noodlebar-toronto.momofuku.com; daily L and D; $$

Ultra-modern, casual Asian eatery with various noodle dishes, plus barbecued pork buns, crispy chicken wings and plenty of vegetarian options. Their desserts, such as the truffle cakes and crack pies, are tasty.

❷ OSGOODE HALL RESTAURANT

130 Queen Street West; tel: 416-947-3361; www.osgoodehallrestaurant.com; Mon–Fri L (Sept–June only); $$

Dine with lawyers taking a break from court under chandeliers and surrounded by stained-glass windows and rows of law books. Local farms supply most of the salad greens, fresh vegetables and meats to complete the Canadiana menu. Try the Upper Canada Club sandwich, served since 1968, or the three-course prix fixe menu.

Art Gallery of Ontario, or AGO

AGO, CHINATOWN AND KENSINGTON MARKET

The Art Gallery of Ontario – the AGO – is one of Toronto's must-see attractions – and it stands near three of the city's most enjoyable neighbourhoods: Chinatown, Kensington Market and Little Italy. All in all, a great day out.

> **DISTANCE:** 2.5km (1.6 miles) walking
> **TIME:** Full day
> **START:** Art Gallery of Ontario
> **END:** Bar Raval
> **POINTS TO NOTE:** The Art Gallery of Ontario (AGO) has variable opening times – so check before you set out. And head out with an appetite, as there will be lots of tempting food options along this route.

As one of Toronto's leading attractions, the **Art Gallery of Ontario** is a major highlight on this tour, even if you only spend an hour or so inside – though you could spend all day here feasting on its magnificent collection. Neighbouring **Chinatown** buzzes with activity, its streets colourfully decorated with large signs of Chinese characters, little curio shops and lots of wonderful sidewalk stands overflowing with exotic fruits and vegetables. No less interesting is the counter-cultural, sometimes gritty neighbourhood of **Kensington Market**. To top off the day,

a few moments or more in **Little Italy** are on the roster, with its fabulous eateries and bars.

ART GALLERY OF ONTARIO

From the St Patrick subway station, walk west on Dundas Street to McCaul Street, where you'll spy the striking modern glass facade of the **Art Gallery of Ontario** (the **AGO**) ❶ (tel: 416-979-6648; www.ago.ca; Tue–Sun 10.30am–5pm, Wed & Fri until 9pm; free Wed 6pm–9pm), designed by Toronto-native architect Frank Gehry and conspicuous amongst the Victorian-era brick row houses and shops.

First opened in 1900 as the Art Museum of Toronto, the AGO has undergone several major renovations over the years, the last as recently as 2018. It is one of the largest art galleries in North America and boasts an impressive collection of Canadian art, as well as works from the Renaissance, African art, and Henry Moore pieces. In addition to its many galleries, the AGO houses a library, art-

Inside the AGO

ist-in-residence spaces, a research centre, lecture hall, a good restaurant, café, coffee shop and gift shop. The AGO also frequently hosts events such as live music, yoga tours and stroller-friendly afternoon tours.

Indigenous and Canadian Art

The compendious **Indigenous and Canadian Art** section holds the core of the AGO's collection, beginning with a small but intriguing assortment of works by eighteenth-century Canadians, most memorably William Berczy's portrait of the Mohawk chief Joseph Brant. The gallery also possesses a fascinating selection of paintings by the intrepid Paul Kane (1810–1871), who ventured deep into the west to draw and paint the tribes of the great plains, and then there are the scenes of colonial life captured by the prolific Cornelius Krieghoff. Later, from the early twentieth century, the AGO owns a comprehensive collection of works by the Group of Seven. The Group, with their profoundly Canadian aesthetic, included the talented Lawren Harris as well as Tom Thomson, one of Canada's most beloved artists, who drowned in a canoeing accident deep in the Ontario backcountry in 1917; Thomson's *West Wind* is perhaps the most famous of all Canadian paintings.

Contemporary Art

The AGO prides itself on its **Contemporary Art** section, which features paintings, sculptures, installations, video and photography from an international assembly of artists from 1960

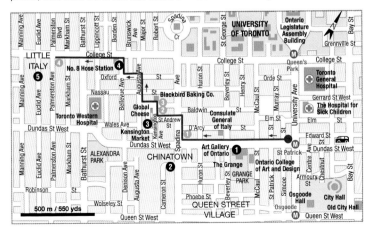

Chinatown on Spadina Avenue

onwards – and from their Canadian rivals and colleagues from 1990. The exhibits are regularly rotated, but prize pieces you can expect to see include Andy Warhol's *Elvis I & II*; Mark Rothko's *No 1 White and Red* and Claes Oldenburg's quirky if somewhat frayed *Giant Hamburger*.

Henry Moore Sculpture Centre

Henry Moore (1898–1986) is best known for his semi-abstract monumental bronze sculptures, one of which was purchased by the City of Toronto in 1965 for the newly inaugurated Nathan Phillips Square (see page 29). Called *The Archer*, this was a controversial purchase due to the cost and abstract nature of the sculpture. This purchase – amongst several factors – led Moore to donate a large collection of his work to the AGO between 1971 and 1974. Today it is the largest public collection of Moore's work in the world, comprising more than 900 bronze and plaster sculptures and works on paper, housed in the dedicated Henry Moore Sculpture Centre on the second floor. Moore is not to everyone's taste – many of his sculptures seem over-blown – and it's hard to gauge whether the AGO now feels grateful for the bequest or saddled with it.

CHINATOWN

Back on Dundas Street West, just beyond the AGO and on the north side of the street, is the start of **Chinatown ❷**, as evidenced by a brigade of cramped stores and vibrant signs. Toronto has several Chinatowns, but this is the largest and it's sometimes referred to as Old Chinatown; it stretches along Dundas Street West and Spadina Avenue. Primarily a Cantonese-speaking neighbourhood, it also includes other Asian-heritage residents, especially Thais, Vietnamese, Indians and Japanese. The first Chinese to settle in Toronto appear to have arrived in the 1870s.

Unusual herb and spice shops, sweet-smelling bakeries, little dim sum restaurants and fresh produce stands overflowing with new foods to try fill the air with exotic scents. Walk toward Spadina Avenue and head north. For lunch, the cash-only, cheap and cheerful **Swatow Restaurant**, see ❶, is an affordable and authentic place to eat. Here you can pick from a range of noodle soups, rice dishes and chow mein.

KENSINGTON MARKET

On the far side of Spadina Avenue, just north of Dundas Street West, lies **Kensington Market ❸**, with its Caribbean flavours, trendy boutiques and friendly cafés. Crossing at St Andrew Street, walk west into the heart of this graffiti-clad bohemian neighbourhood, which is now a National Historic Site of Canada.

Bohemian Kensington Market

Kensington Gems

Blackbird Baking Co.

172 Baldwin Street; tel: 416-546-2280;
www.blackbirdbakingco.com

A fantastic bakery that produces amazing sourdough breads, among other baked treats, both savoury and sweet, including granola, lemon tarts and scones. Try one of the take-out sandwiches, too.

Cocktail Emporium

20 Kensington Avenue; tel: 647-729-9986; www.cocktailemporium.com

For the finest barware plus fun tiki decor and crucial cocktail ingredients, this bright shop is exactly what you need for anything drink and cocktail related.

Courage My Love

14 Kensington Avenue; tel: 416-979-1992

Possibly the best vintage shop around, with lovingly hand-picked items spanning decades of retro styles from around the globe. Find cowboy boots, flared pants, vintage purses, buttons and beads, plus housewares and other unique trinkets.

House of Spice

190 Augusta Avenue; tel: 416-593-9724;
www.ehouseofspice.com

Selling herbs and spices from around the world since the early 1970s, this little family-owned shop can be sniffed out from miles away. Coffees, teas, hot sauces and sea salts also make up part of their exotic collection.

One of the city's most celebrated neighbourhoods, Kensington Market is bordered by College Street in the north, Dundas Street West to the south, Spadina Avenue to the east, and Bathurst Street to the west. Eclectic to say the least, it is an edgy melting pot of cultures, coloured by street art, with wafts of spice, barbecue, and sweet pastries filling the narrow streets. Vintage stores spill their wares along the sidewalks where friendly, easy-going locals and wide-eyed visitors peruse the unusual goods on offer.

Kensington Market has always been home to a varied group of Torontonians, first as a Jewish community in the 1930s, then waves of Caribbean immigrants in the 1950s called the area their new home, as did American political refugees in the 1970s during the Vietnam War. Today it's an amazing mix of European, Middle Eastern, Latin American, and Asian cultures, all blending together in, at times, a rather odd but wonderful fashion. Where else could you go for both Hungarian and Thai food under one roof? Yes, you can have that pork schnitzel with your pad thai noodles.

During the summer months, the whole area goes car-free on the last Sunday of the month (Pedestrian Sundays: from May until October), and visitors are treated to live and entertaining performances, farmers' markets with myriad food trucks, and plenty of great people watching.

Seven Lives Tacos   *Exploring Kensington Market*

Turning north onto narrow Kensington Avenue, Global Cheese, at no.76, is a must stop for picnic goodies. Or grab a quick bite from **Rasta Pasta**, see ②, offering Jamaican-fusion or **Seven Lives Tacos**, see ③, for Mexican tacos, right next door.

Continue onto neighbouring Baldwin Street and its cluster of varied eateries, before proceeding onto Augusta Avenue, then strolling north to Oxford Street, passing by the **Blue Banana Market**, at no.250, an excellent shop for unusual gifts and souvenirs ranging from kids clothing to Québec-produced maple syrup.

NO. 8 FIRE HOSE STATION

Heading west along Oxford Street, turn north onto Bellevue Avenue. Here, at the corner of College Street and Bellevue, you'll see a modest red-brick fire hall. Called **No. 8 Fire Hose Station** ④, it was originally built in 1878, with a clock tower that was added in 1899. The eight-story tower had a lookout at the top for the firefighters, and the hoses were hung to dry from here as well. In 1911, the fire hall received the first motorized fire truck in the city, replacing the horse-drawn fire wagons. It is one of the oldest, still-existing fire halls in the city.

Now you can either take the College Street streetcar westbound or walk a few more blocks west toward the Little Italy neighbourhood, which officially starts at Bathurst Street and College Street.

LITTLE ITALY

Centred along College Street, between Bathurst Street and Ossington Avenue, Toronto's **Little Italy** ⑤, is known for its inviting trattorias, lively pizzerias and excellent espresso bars. Toronto's most delicious street festival is cele-

No. 8 Fire Hose Station's tower

The Taste of Little Italy festival attracts the crowds

brated here, 'Taste of Little Italy', transforming the area into one huge street party every June. Make sure to visit the area if you're traveling in Toronto then.

However, this neighbourhood is not distinctly Italian, as the name (and festival) might suggest. At least not so much as it used to be during its heyday in the 1950s. Over the last five decades, those of Portuguese and Latin American heritage have set up home and shop in Little Italy, also bringing with them all the wonderful flavours and styles of their respective cultures in the form of bakeries, boutiques and

taco shops. During that time, another Italian enclave, called **Corso Italia**, just 4km (2.5 miles) north of Little Italy, along St Clair Avenue West, has prospered and is now considered Toronto's second Little Italy.

Little Italy isn't just about pizzerias, cafés, and trattorias though. It's also humming with some of the best bars in the entire city. Although not Italian, enjoy dinner at the Spanish **Bar Raval**, see ❹, at College Street and Palmerston Boulevard. This popular spot serves excellent tapas and sparkling cocktails.

Food and Drink

❶ SWATOW RESTAURANT
309 Spadina Avenue; tel: 416-977-0601; www.swatowrestauranttoronto.com; daily L and D; $
Inexpensive and straightforward Chinese spot for fast, excellent and generous portions of noodle soup, fried rice dishes, and other comfort Cantonese foods. It's open late, but note that they accept cash only.

❷ RASTA PASTA
61 Kensington Avenue; tel: 647-501-4505; www.eatrastapasta.ca; Tue–Sun L; $
A Kensington Market staple with long line-ups to prove it, this Jamaican take-out counter is famous for its jerk chicken. Try it in The Vatican – a grilled panini stuffed with

home-made, two-day marinated jerk chicken and fresh coleslaw.

❸ SEVEN LIVES TACOS
72 Kensington Avenue; tel: 416-393-4636; www.sevenlivesto.ca; daily L; $
Tiny and always busy Mexican take-out spot serving some of the best California and Baja-style tacos in the city. Note that this is a cash-only establishment.

❹ BAR RAVAL
505 College Street; tel: 647-344-8001; www.thisisbarraval.com; daily L and D; $$$
This is a simply fantastic and very casual Spanish tapas bar – the seafood is a treat – and it features a gorgeous Gaudí-inspired interior. There's also a heated and covered patio space.

Kayaking between the Toronto Islands

TORONTO ISLANDS

It's a quick and pleasant passenger ferry ride from the centre of the city to the Toronto Islands, a leafy, car-free archipelago, where cycle and footpaths thread through lovely tranquil parkland.

DISTANCE: 10km (6 miles) walking and passenger ferry
TIME: Half day
START/END: Jack Layton Ferry Terminal
POINTS TO NOTE: Ferry tickets are for a return trip and can be purchased at the terminal or online (the best option if you want to avoid the line). Ferries depart approximately every 15 minutes during the summer months. The one way journey takes about 15 minutes. There's also the option of chartering a boat, water taxi, or even taking a kayak or canoe across, though swimming is definitely not advised due to dangerous conditions. No cars are allowed on the islands, but you can take bikes and strollers on the ferry, though during the very busy summer season bikes may be refused, so call ahead to check. While there are a few restaurants and snack bars on the islands, we recommend bringing a picnic lunch, perhaps picked out from the nearby St Lawrence Market see page 38.

Originally a sandbar peninsula, the Toronto Islands, which arch around the city's harbour, were cut adrift from the mainland by a violent storm in 1858. First used as a breezy summer retreat by the Mississauga Nation, the islands went through various incarnations in the 20th century – they once held a baseball stadium, where the legendary Babe Ruth hit his first professional run, and hosted fun fairs with horses diving into the lake from the pier. Nowadays, they are inhabited by a spirited group of individualists intent on preserving the islands' rustic charms: visitors' cars are banned and many locals use wheelbarrows or golf buggies to move their wares around.

All in all, the Toronto Islands are simply delightful, a semi-rustic hidey-hole comprising around fifteen islands with the biggest and most developed being Centre Island. The latter possesses amusement arcades and the pocket-sized Toronto City Airport, though this cannot be accessed from the islands – the airport is serviced by a different ferry system (and tunnel), at the foot of Bathurst Street.

A world away from the bustle of the city

Most restaurants and attractions are closed during the winter months, though the ferries operate year-round, give or take the occasional interruption by winter storms. Cross-country skiing, snowshoeing, and ice-skating are just some of the activities happening during the wintertime.

JACK LAYTON FERRY TERMINAL

From the **Jack Layton Ferry Terminal** (tel: 416-392-8193; www.toronto. ca; daily departures), just east of the Westin Harbour Castle Hotel at the foot of Bay Street and Queen's Quay, three public passenger ferries shuttle across to the Toronto Islands every day. Each follows a separate route, but since all the islands are connected, it doesn't really matter which ferry you take, though the most popular one is the ferry to the family-friendly Centre Island.

CENTRE ISLAND

After getting off the ferry, there's an information booth where you can pick up a map of the islands. **Centre Island ❶** (tel: 416-392-8193; www.

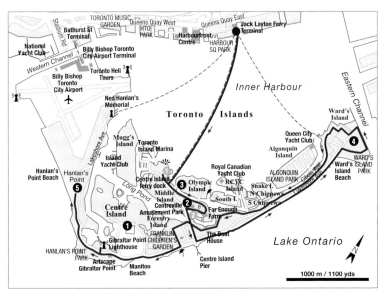

The pier on Centre Island

centreisland.ca), the largest island of all, has several dining options, or, if you packed a picnic, head to the large park areas or the sandy beach. There are a few playgrounds as well, splash and wading pools, a Frisbee golf course, a maze, landscaped gardens, beaches, plus places to rent bicycles and boats. Small children will especially enjoy spending some time at the **Franklin Children's Garden**. Based on the *Franklin the Turtle* stories, it has storytelling and kids' gardening sessions, statues of book characters,

Fun times at the Centreville Amusement Park

a playhouse, and a 'snail trail' leading to a great viewpoint.

The **Toronto Island BBQ & Beer** restaurant, see ❶, immediately northwest of the ferry dock has fantastic views from its large patio. You could have lunch there or head back later for dinner.

CENTREVILLE AMUSEMENT PARK

The highlight for many families on Centre Island is the **Centreville Amusement Park** ❷ (tel: 416-203-0405; www.centreisland.ca; May–Sept, hours vary), which is just northwest of the ferry docks. This is a vintage-style amusement park with a Ferris wheel, carousel, miniature railway, swan ride, log flume and a petting zoo. The park is free to wander around, but the rides require tickets. There are several snack bars for quick bites to eat here, or try the casual **Carousel Café**, see ❷.

Heading to the Islands

All together, the islands cover 242 hectares (600 acres) and each island is connected to a network of pedestrian and bicycle-friendly paved paths, wooden boardwalks and bridges. It makes for a lovely day away from the hustle and bustle of the city, and includes memorable views back over the city centre as a bonus.

View back towards the city from Centre Island

OLYMPIC ISLAND

Olympic Island ❸, accessed via a brace of dinky foot bridges from Centre Island, offers leafy, well-kept parkland and outstanding panoramic views of the downtown Toronto skyline.

WARD'S ISLAND

Heading south from the Centreville Amusement Park, cross the bridge and then head east, passing between the cedar-hedge maze and **The Boat House** rental shop. This is now considered **Ward's Island** ❹. Actually a peninsula attached to Centre Island, Ward's is a residential area with beautiful gardens and quiet streets lined with several-hundred immaculate cottages dating back to the 1920s. The beaches north and on the eastern-most tip are sandy and simply wonderful. There are no restaurants or shops on Ward's. It does, however, have a flying disc (Frisbee) golf course, several playgrounds and a soccer field.

HANLAN'S POINT

Doubling back from Ward's Island, track west to the **Gibraltar Point Lighthouse** (no public access), a neat and trim brick structure, which dates from 1808. The first keeper here met an untimely end: in a quarrel over bootlegged liquor with two British soldiers from Fort Toronto, he was murdered and then, it is believed, chopped up and buried. Stories that the lighthouse is haunted have been around ever since. Beyond the lighthouse lies **Hanlan's Point** ❺, a rather bleak and largely treeless expanse, which is best known for its clothing-optional beach – **Hanlan's Point Beach**.

Food and Drink

❶ TORONTO ISLAND BBQ & BEER
Centre Island; tel: 416-504-4841; www.torontoislandbbq.com; Mon–Fri 11.30am–8pm, Sat–Sun 11.30am–9.30pm, June–Sept; $$
Casual waterside eatery with some of best views of Toronto's skyline, especially from the capacious patio. Specialties include smoked meats, poutine, burgers, and sandwiches, plus there's a kids' menu and, of course, plenty of beer on tap.

❷ CAROUSEL CAFÉ
Centre Island; tel: 416-203-0405; www.centreisland.ca; daily 11am–5pm, Apr–Oct; $$
Relaxed café within the Centreville Amusement Park serving pub fare such as burgers, sandwiches, pastas, and fish and chips. They also have a kids' menu and a sunny outdoor patio.

The extravagant Casa Loma

NORTH TORONTO – CASA LOMA AND VICINITY

Casa Loma and the Spadina Museum are a contrasting pair of historic houses – one a grand folly, the other demure and discrete – that form the backbone of this route, which culminates in Koreatown, with its authentic eateries and karaoke bars.

DISTANCE: 3km (1.9 miles) walking or partly by bus
TIME: Full day
START: Casa Loma
END: Korean Village Restaurant
POINTS TO NOTE: Both the Tollkeeper's Cottage and the Spadina Museum have limited opening hours – check before you set out; entrance to the latter is also by guided tour only. Getting to Casa Loma, say from Union Station, is simple. Just take Subway line 1 northbound to Dupont Station, then proceed north along Spadina Road for about 5 minutes, climb the steps and you'll reach the castle.

Toronto is liberally sprinkled with historic architecture. There are the old barracks at Fort York (see page 34) and the sturdy brick warehouses of the Distillery Historic District (see page 42), plus a veritable brigade of pretty Victorian homes scattered around the city's older neighbourhoods. Cream of the crop, however, are Casa Loma, a grand folly if ever there was one, and the adjacent Spadina Museum, an intriguing insight into the tastes of the city's haute bourgeoisie – and a striking contrast to its garish neighbour. Round off the day by dropping by the modest Tollkeeper's Cottage and by grabbing a bite to eat in Koreatown.

CASA LOMA

Casa Loma ❶ (tel: 416-923-1171; www.casaloma.ca; daily 9.30am–5pm) is undoubtedly Toronto's most bizarre attraction, an enormous towered and turreted mansion built for Sir Henry Pellatt between 1911 and 1914. Every inch the self-made man, Pellatt was determined to construct a house no one could ignore, even importing Scottish stonemasons to build the wall around his property. He spent more than $3m fulfilling his dream, but business misfortunes forced him to move out in 1923. His legacy is a strange mixture of medieval fantasy and early twentieth-century technology: secret passageways, an elevator, and claustrophobic wood-panelled rooms baffled by gargantuan pipes and plumbing.

A clearly numbered, self-guiding route

Lady Pellatt's suite, painted in Wedgwood blue

goes up one side of the house and down the other. It begins on the ground floor in the Great Hall, a pseudo-Gothic extravaganza with an 18m-high cross-beamed ceiling, a Wurlitzer organ and enough floor space to accommodate several hundred guests.

Spare time also for the terraced gardens, which tumble down the ridge at the back of the house. They are parcelled up into several different sections and easily explored along a network of footpaths, beginning on the terrace behind the great hall.

SPADINA MUSEUM

Right next door to Casa Loma, at 285 Spadina Road, is the **Spadina Museum** ❷ (tel: 416-392-6910; www.toronto.ca; by guided tours only, hours vary), offering a glimpse of domestic life in Toronto through the lens of the Austin family from 1900 to 1930. The site includes six structures, one of which is the main three-story house built in 1866 with original furnishings. The interior of the house and outbuildings can be seen by guided tour only, though the Victorian-Edwardian gardens are open to the public and visitors are free to wander there.

The property was originally purchased in 1866

by businessman and financier James Austin, originally from Northern Ireland and founder of the Dominion Bank, known today as the Toronto-Dominion Bank, or TD. At first, Austin and his family farmed the land, and later subdivided it and sold the majority of it off, keeping under 6 acres that included an orchard, grape arbour, a kitchen garden, and the English-style formal lawns and borders.

The historic main house illustrates the change of art, decor, technologies, and architecture from the 1860s through the 1930s, including Victorian, Edwardian, Arts and Crafts, Art Deco, and Colonial Revival styles.

TOLLKEEPER'S COTTAGE

From the Spadina Museum, walk west down Austin Terrace, veering south (left) down Walmer Road before then turning right along Davenport Road to Bathurst

Korean bibimbap   *Koreatown, Bloor Street*

Street – allow about 12 minutes. Metres from the Davenport/Bathurst intersection stands the **Tollkeeper's Cottage** ❸ (tel: 416-515-7546; www.tollkeeper-scottage.ca; times vary; by donation) – one of the oldest homes in the city, built in 1835. It's now a small museum with sparse period furnishings reflecting the simple times of the toll collector.

For lunch, walk south down Bathurst Street from the cottage, turning east onto Dupont Street, to the corner of Dupont and Howland Avenue where **Schmaltz Appetizing**, see ❶, offers Jewish deli items such as the classic bagel with cream cheese and lox.

KOREATOWN

From Bathurst Street and Dupont Street, catch the number 7 bus southbound or walk for about 1.5km (1 mile) south to Bloor Street West. You're now in **Koreatown** ❹ – a vibrant little neighbourhood full of inexpensive eateries, karaoke bars, and novelty gift shops, ending at the large Christie Pits Park. Toronto is justifiably famous for its neighbourhoods – Chinatown, Little Italy and so forth – but Koreatown is one of the most engaging.

Toronto has about 50,000 people living in the city that identify themselves as having a Korean heritage, some of whom have opened up businesses around **Koreatown** – a small stretch along Bloor Street, between Christie and Bathurst Streets. Restaurants and bakeries serving authentic Korean fare, novelty gift shops with imported Korean goods and grocery stores carrying specialty Korean products can all be found in Koreatown. Most of the city's karaoke bars have opened up here. To experience the full flavour of this neighbourhood, the annual Korean Dano Spring Festival in June, with its martial arts demonstrations and traditional music, is a great opportunity to enjoy more of Korea's culture in Toronto.

End the day with an authentic Korean meal at the **Korean Village Restaurant**, see ❷.

Food and Drink

❶ **SCHMALTZ APPETIZING**
414 Dupont Street; tel: 647-350-4261; www.schmaltzappetizing.com; daily B and L; $
Jewish deli in The Annex neighbourhood with fantastic, easy-on-the-budget bagel sandwiches filled with whipped cream cheese, freshly sliced lox, capers and onions. Eat inside or enjoy it out on their little patio.

❷ **KOREAN VILLAGE RESTAURANT**
628 Bloor Street West; tel: 416-536-0290; www.koreanvillagetoronto.com; daily L and D; $$
A staple of Koreatown, this homey, family-run authentic Korean restaurant has a choice of private rooms and booth seating. Ask for the table BBQ for a traditional and fun way to cook your own food.

Cheetah love at the Toronto Zoo

TORONTO WITH KIDS

Plodding the streets of Toronto may soon stir resistance from your average child, but few will object to a longer excursion out to the exemplary Toronto Zoo. Two obvious alternatives – each a day-long excursion in its own right – are the Ontario Science Centre and Canada's Wonderland.

DISTANCE: 64km (40 miles) driving or subway and bus
TIME: Full day
START/END: Toronto Zoo
POINTS TO NOTE: The Toronto Zoo is a two-hour ride northeast with public transportation, starting from Union Station on line 1 (Finch direction) to Bloor-Yonge Station, then on line 2 east to Kennedy Station, and then the 86A bus directly to the zoo. Driving will take about 40 minutes.

Depending on how far you feel like travelling with the kids, there are options of family-friendly attractions throughout the downtown area and farther out. A day trip to the Toronto Islands (see page 55) makes for a wonderful, family-friendly outing, provided the weather is cooperating. Back on the mainland, the CN Tower (see page 36) offers a thrilling elevator ride to the top, with views that will blow kids' minds. Down on the ground again, Ripley's Aquarium of Canada (see page 28) is perfect on a rainy day, while an afternoon at the Royal Ontario Museum (see page 30) with its dinosaur displays and eerie bat cave will further satisfy little naturalists.

For mini sports enthusiasts, the Hockey Hall of Fame (see page 38) with its competitive games and hockey treasures will provide at least an hour or two or fun. Casa Loma (see page 59) can be interesting to older children who'll appreciate the secret passageways, towers, and antique stables and even Fort York (see page 34), with its costumed staff and re-enactments, can easily fill up an hour or two.

For an out-of-town attraction, the Toronto Zoo is well worth the drive. A whole day can be easily spent here, with not only animals to see but also rides to go on, a splash zone to play in, and an interesting Wildlife Health Centre to visit where visitors can catch a behind-the-scenes glimpse of the work done there. Similarly engaging is the Ontario Science Centre, which is ideal for pre-teens, or you can abandon education altogether and opt for the rollercoaster rides of Canada's Wonderland.

Playground in High Park *A Siberian tiger at the Toronto Zoo*

TORONTO ZOO

The **Toronto Zoo** ❶ (tel: 416-392-5911; www.torontozoo.com; daily 9am–7pm, earlier closures in winter) is the largest zoo in Canada, and one of the largest in North America at 710 acres (287 hectares), and features a varied terrain, from dense forest, to valleys, rivers and savanna.

The zoo, which is modelled partly on the famous San Diego Zoo, is divided into seven zoogeographic regions, with over 5,000 animals representing over 450 species housed in tropical pavilions and natural outdoor environments. All the exciting species are here, including

apes, tigers, leopards, lions, rhinos, hippos, meerkats, komodo dragons, camels, pandas, polar bears, and raptors, plus many more interesting creatures, and a selection of Canadian wildlife.

6 miles (10km) of walking trails crisscross the zoo, or you can hop on the Zoomobile if walking becomes too much. Strollers and wagons are available for rent as well. Lots of snack bars

Petting the llamas at the High Park Zoo

Free Family Fun

High Park

Tel: 416-338-0338; www.highparktoronto.com; llama pens Sat–Sun 11.30am–2pm

This lakefront, 161-hectare (400-acre) park west of Toronto's downtown core has a free zoo with llamas, which you can feed and pet, and various other child-friendly animals. The park also has several playgrounds, snack bars, ponds, lots of trails, a museum, an outdoor pool, and a nature centre.

Riverdale Farm

Tel: 416-392-6794; www.riverdalefarm toronto.ca; daily 9am–5pm; free

Located in the Cabbagetown neighbourhood, northeast of downtown Toronto, is the Riverdale Farm. This is a 3-hectare (7.4-acre) working farm, originally on the site of a zoo that began in 1888. The farm is free and open to the public year-round, and features chickens, goats, pigs, sheep, cows, horses, donkeys, and more, some of which can be petted and fed.

Cheetah love at the Toronto Zoo

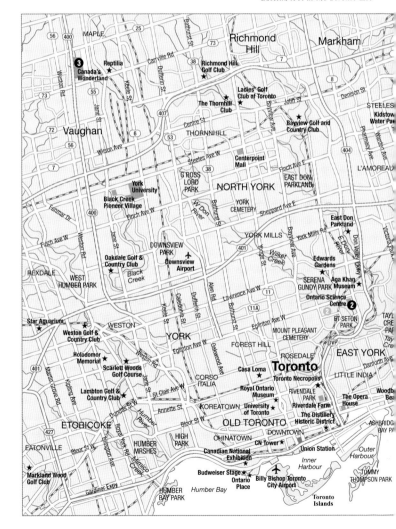

A family explores exhibits at the Ontario Science Centre

and restaurants are onsite and the zoo allows you to bring in your own food as well, with picnic tables set out at various locations. **Smoke's Poutinerie**, see ①, has two locations in the zoo, one in the Front Courtyard just north of the main entrance, and one just outside of the African Savanna region.

ONTARIO SCIENCE CENTRE

The **Ontario Science Centre** ② (tel: 416-696-1000; www.ontariosciencecentre.ca; daily 10am–5pm, Sat until 8pm) is a splendid science museum located about 11km (7 miles) northeast of downtown Toronto, with over 800 interactive, high-tech exhibits that the whole family can enjoy. Highlights include a rainfor-

Ontario Science Centre

Canada's Wonderland, a fun day out

est complete with poison dart frogs, a touchable tornado, a cave, and a coral reef, amazing larger-than-life art installations and meteorites from Mars. There's also an indoor rock-climbing wall and an IMAX theatre that shows nature films on a giant dome screen.

For dining options, the Science Centre has several cafés and restaurants on site, offering the standard fare of snacks such as pastries, sandwiches, salads, burgers, hot dogs, and pizza. If you've driven out here, try heading west, about 2.4km (1.5 miles), to **Conspiracy Pizza**, see ❷. Feast on an array of interesting pizza toppings and enjoy a selection of chili lime oven roasted chicken wings on the side.

CANADA'S WONDERLAND

A must for thrill-seekers, **Canada's Wonderland** ❸ (tel: 905-832-8131; www. canadaswonderland.com; daily 10am–10pm June–Sept) is a huge amusement park an hour's drive north of Toronto. As well as your favourite cartoon characters wandering around, it features over 60 rides, a water park, miniature golf, an arcade and plenty more.

The park is divided up into nine zones, with three zones dedicated to younger visitors, but the wild rollercoasters are found throughout. The Yukon Striker, new in 2019, is the world's fastest, tallest, and longest dive coaster – the type with a near-vertical drop that's definitely not for the faint-hearted!

The park has a hatful of cafés, snack shacks and eateries to keep you stuffed and satisfied all day long. And if you are here all day, you may want to consider purchasing an All Day Dining Plan that allows you to eat a meal at each of the participating restaurants for one relatively low price.

Food and Drink

❶ SMOKE'S POUTINERIE

Toronto Zoo; tel: 416-392-5929; www.smokespoutinerie.com; daily B, L, and D; $
A Toronto original, this poutinerie chain is fast becoming a national hit, for fries covered in gravy and cheese curds, that is. Try the Double Pork poutine with chipotle pulled pork and double-smoked bacon. No need for seconds after this satisfying dish.

❷ CONSPIRACY PIZZA

176 Wicksteed Avenue; tel: 647-694-3327; www.conspiracypizza.ca; Wed–Thu & Sun 11.30am–9pm, Fri–Sat 11.30am–10pm; $$
You will be treated to a wide selection of pizzas here with some interesting names. The 'Chupacabra' pizza, for example, features mozzarella, Manchego cheese, chorizo sausage, red onion and mushroom. There are plenty of vegetarian choices, white sauce-based pizzas, and plant-based eaters can enjoy vegan chorizo. Make the most of the patio, too.

The mighty falls

NIAGARA FALLS

Ontario's one must-see attraction is Niagara Falls, a thunderous, world-famous waterfall. You can choose to go for the day – it's within easy striking distance of Toronto – or spend a night in the area, exploring its wineries and the charms of Niagara-on-the-Lake.

DISTANCE: 260km (161 miles) return trip driving or public transportation from downtown Toronto, 50km (31 miles) driving within Niagara Falls and surrounding area.

TIME: Full day to two days

START: Niagara Falls

END: Château des Charmes

POINTS TO NOTE: It takes about 1.5 hours to drive from downtown Toronto to Niagara Falls, following the QEW (Queen Elizabeth Way) highway. Buses connect Toronto to Burlington and to Niagara Falls daily, and it takes about 2.5 hours. GO Train has a seasonal daily train service which runs from Union Station to Niagara Falls Train Station. Alternatively, VIA Rail offers an all-year-round service from Toronto to Niagara Falls. Trains depart twice daily or so and takes around two hours one way. Niagara Falls Train Station is about 4km (2.5 miles) from the falls so you need to take a bus or taxi from there. Consult the accommodations listings (see page 105) for hotel and motel options in Niagara Falls and Niagara-on-the-Lake.

If you have your own transportation, you may want to consider exploring the area outside the town of Niagara Falls, most notably **Niagara-on-the-Lake**, a lovely little historic town, and there are several prime **wineries** that merit a visit hereabouts also.

NIAGARA FALLS

Formed at the end of the last Ice Age, about 12,000 years ago, **Niagara Falls ❶** (www.niagaraparks.com) actually consists of three falls – Horseshoe Falls, the American Falls and the Bridal Veil Falls – that straddle the international border between Canada and the USA; they can all be viewed for free along the extended promenade that runs along the Canada side. Niagara Falls is also the namesake city in which the falls reside, a medium-sized Canadian town that is strikingly tacky but colourful with casinos, sleazy motels and tourist traps.

The views of the falls are, thankfully, best appreciated from the Canadian side, and are at their wildest in

Having fun on a boat tour

the late spring and early summer. The Horseshoe Falls are the mightiest and are 57 metres (188ft) high and 790 metres (2,600ft) wide. During the winter, ice formations on the falls are often spectacular and the crowds have disappeared. The falls are illuminated in a rainbow of colours every evening, from dusk until late, certainly one reason to stick around for a night. Fireworks shows, right above the falls, are held nightly beginning at 10pm in the summer, then just on weekends and special holidays throughout the rest of the year.

There are many exciting ways to experience the falls on your travels. Board one of the **Hornblower Cruises** (tel: 1-855-264-2427; daily May–Nov; www.niagara cruises.com) to get up close to the falls, feel the mist and hear the thundering roar, as this boat trip takes you on a 700-passenger vessel right into the spray of the

Horseshoe Falls

falls. Prices include a mist poncho as you will get wet.

For a self-guided walk alongside the rapids, there's the **White Water Walk** (daily mid-Apr–early Nov). Or to see them from above you can board the **Whirlpool Aero Car**, a historic cable car offering spectacular views plus a ride children will particularly enjoy. You can even zip-line across the rapids; all details are on the website – www.niagaraparks.com.

Several tour companies offer excursions from Toronto to Niagara Falls. One of the best is **King Tours** (tel: 416-315-4065; www.kingtours.ca) with daily departures. Tours last the full day and guests are picked up from their hotel in the morning. Stops include Niagara-on-the-Lake plus a winery visit and tasting. Add-ons can be included, such as a lunch or a cruise tour.

TABLE ROCK WELCOME CENTRE

A visit to the **Table Rock Welcome Centre ❷** (tel: 905-358-3268; www.niagaraparks.com; Mon–Fri 9am–5pm, Sat–Sun 9am–8pm) is a good starting point when arriving in the city of Niagara Falls. Located right beside the falls, this complex has several attractions, such as Niagara's Fury, a 4D simulation of the creation of the falls, and the Journey Behind the Falls, where visitors descend down 46 metres (151ft) by elevator and get in behind and below the falls. The centre also has a food court, gift shops and an information booth. For a quick bite to eat, especially if breakfast was skipped or hurried that morning, pop into the **Flying Saucer**, see ❶, about 10 minutes drive west of the centre – yes, it's as bizarre as it sounds.

BOTANICAL GARDENS & BUTTERFLY CONSERVATORY

Established in 1936, the **Botanical Gardens ❸** (tel: 905-356-8119; www.niagaraparks.com; daily dawn until dusk; free) consists of over 40 hectares (100 acres) of beautifully landscaped gardens filled with roses, herbs and manicured hedges. The **Butterfly Conservatory ❹** (tel: 905-358-0025; www.niagaraparks.com; daily 10am–7pm) is located within the gardens and introduces visitors to a tropical paradise full of lush plants and thousands of free-flying butterflies.

NIAGARA-ON-THE-LAKE

Hugging the shores of Lake Ontario, the charming town of **Niagara-on-the-Lake ❺** is just 23km (14 miles) north of Niagara Falls. Much less kitschy than Niagara Falls, it's famous for its well-preserved, colonial-style buildings, which line up along its short main streets, primarily Queen and Johnson streets, with a distinctive clock tower at the centre. A popular tourist destination, Niagara-on-the-Lake has a

Niagara-on-the-Lake

brigade of gift shops and cafés and is also home to one of the best theatre festivals in Ontario, the annual **Shaw Festival** (tel 1-800-511-7429; www. shawfest.com). In normal times, the festival runs from April to November and there are performances in all four of the town's theatres; this is the only festival in the world devoted solely to the works of George Bernard Shaw and his contemporaries.

For lunch or dinner, enjoy true farm-to-table fare at **Treadwell Cuisine**, see ❷; for accommodation here, see page 105.

Niagara Facts

The falls are only about 12,000 years old, created by glacial run-off at the end of the last ice age.

American daredevil Nik Wallenda crossed the falls on a tightrope in 2012, the first person to do this since 1896. The very first person to successfully cross was French tightrope walker Charles Blondin, who did it in 1859 – and on many subsequent occasions.

The first person to go over the falls in a barrel and survive was 63-year-old Annie Edson Taylor, who completed her daredevil stunt in 1901 – though she did take the precaution of using a custom-made oak and iron barrel.

The Horseshoe Falls have frozen over just once, but the American Falls have frozen over six times.

FORT GEORGE

On the edge of Niagara-on-the-Lake, a five- to ten-minute walk east of the town's clock tower via Picton Street, is the splendidly restored **Fort George** ❻ (tel: 905-468-6614; www.pc.gc.ca; May–Oct daily 10am–5pm), a one-time British military outpost built in the 1790s. Allow a couple of hours to explore the fort, which was one of a line of stockades slung across the Great Lakes to protect Canada from the US. The original stockade was destroyed during the War of 1812 and the site lay deserted until it was thoroughly excavated and the fort reconstructed in the 1930s. Today, the palisaded compound with its protective bastions holds about a dozen buildings, among them the officers' quarters and two log blockhouses, which doubled as soldiers' barracks. The difference between the quarters and the barracks is striking. The former are comparatively spacious and were once – as recorded on shipping lists – furnished with fancy knick-knacks, while the latter housed the men and some of their wives (six wives out of every hundred were allowed to join the garrison) in the meanest of conditions. A tunnel links the main part of the fort with one of the exterior bastions, or ravelins, which is itself the site of a third, even stronger blockhouse. The only original building is the powder magazine of 1796, its interior equipped with wood and copper fittings to reduce the

Fort George

chances of an accidental explosion; as an added precaution, the soldiers working here went barefoot. There are also ninety-minute lantern-light **ghost tours** of the fort – good fun with or without an apparition (tel: 905-468-6621; www.niagaraghosts.com). Tours begin at the car park in front of the fort; further details on their website.

INNISKILLIN WINES AND CHÂTEAU DES CHARMES

Heading back out from Niagara-on-the-Lake, stop at **Inniskillin Wines** ❼ (tel: 905-468-2187; www.inniskillin.com; daily 10am–6pm May–Oct, Mon–Sat 10am–5pm Nov–Apr; free tours), a historic and pioneering winery famous for its icewine and range of table wines. Inniskillin also has a seasonal eatery, serving smoked and grilled meats for lunch at the **Inniskillin Market Grill & Smokehouse**, see ❸.

Before heading back to Toronto, visit the winery of **Château des Charmes** ❽ (tel: 905-262-4219; www.fromthebosc family.com; daily 10am–6pm). Known for its chardonnay, this winery has gorgeous grounds to stroll around.

Food and Drink

❶ FLYING SAUCER

6768 Lundy's Lane, Niagara Falls; tel: 905-356-4553; www.flyingsaucerrestaurant.com; daily B, L, and D; $

Cheap and incredibly cheerful, this is not just a touristy, sci-fi themed diner – the food is 'out of this world' – but the locals love it too, especially the kids. The early bird breakfast special here is just $4 with the purchase of a drink, and includes two eggs, home fries and toast.

❷ TREADWELL CUISINE

114 Queen Street, Niagara-on-the-Lake; tel: 905-934-9797; www.treadwellcuisine.com; daily L and D; $$$

This classy but relaxed restaurant proudly showcases fresh, seasonal and local

ingredients through its delectable Canadian menu. The Lobster Club sandwich with sun-dried tomato and whipped goat cheese is incredible. They have a bakery across the lane and its perfect for bringing fresh goodies back.

❸ INNISKILLIN MARKET GRILL & SMOKEHOUSE

1499 Line 3 Niagara Parkway; tel: 905-468-2187; www.inniskillin.com; 11am–4pm daily July–Sept 3, May–June and Sept 4–Oct Sat–Sun only; $$

Poutines, grilled and smoked meats, sandwiches, salads and oysters are on the seasonal menu at this picturesque lunch spot. Try the Inniskillin Ice Cream Sandwich for dessert – a double chocolate brownie with vanilla ice cream, topped with a non-alcoholic Cabernet Franc syrup.

KINGSTON HIGHLIGHTS

The historic city of Kingston is the most enticing of the communities that lie dotted along the northern shore of Lake Ontario. Exploring the city is a real pleasure – and you can take a cruise through the Thousand Islands from here, too.

DISTANCE: Morning cruise through the Thousand Islands plus 7km (4.4 miles) walking

TIME: Full day

START: Confederation Park

END: Le Chien Noir

POINTS TO NOTE: It takes a little under 3 hours to travel from Toronto to Kingston along Hwy 401, a distance of around 260km (162 miles). VIA rail connects Toronto with Kingston too; it's a relatively frequent service that takes about 3 hours, but Kingston rail station is located just off John Counter Boulevard (and near Hwy 2), an inconvenient 7km northwest of the city centre. Kingston can also be used as a handy stopping off point on the longer journey between Toronto and Ottawa (646km/400miles). The second leg of this longer journey – between Kingston and Ottawa – is most scenically done along the Rideau Canal (see page 75). If you are looking for hotel options in Kingston, see page 106.

Central Kingston's medley of old buildings displays every architectural foible admired by the Victorians, from neo-Gothic mansions with high gables and perky dormer windows to elegant Italianate villas. The cream of the stylistic crop are the city's neoclassical limestone buildings, especially City Hall and the Cathedral of St George. Kingston also holds the first-rate Agnes Etherington Art Centre gallery and Bellevue House, once the home of Prime Minister Sir John A. Macdonald. Add to this a cluster of good restaurants and scenic boat trips round the Thousand Islands just offshore, and you have a city that is well worth visiting.

CONFEDERATION PARK

The obvious place to start a visit to Kingston is pocket-sized **Confederation Park ❶**, where manicured lawns run behind the harbour with its marina and squat, nineteenth-century Martello fortified tower. The park marks the site of the original French fur-trading post established here as Fort Frontenac in 1673. It was not a success, but struggled on

Skyline of Kingston

until 1758 when it fell to a combined force of British, Americans and Iroquois, a victory soon followed by an influx of United Empire Loyalists, who promptly developed Kingston – as they renamed it – into a major shipbuilding centre and naval base. The money poured in and the future looked rosy when the completion of the Rideau Canal (see page 75), linking Kingston with Ottawa in 1832, opened up its hinterland. Kingston became Canada's capital in 1841 and although it lost this distinction just three years later it remained the region's most important town until the end of the nineteenth century. In recent years, Kingston – and its 140,000 inhabitants – has had as many economic downs as ups, but it does benefit from the presence of Queen's University, one of Canada's most prestigious academic institutions, and of the Royal Military College, the country's answer to Sandhurst and West Point.

THOUSAND ISLANDS CRUISE

Beside Confederation Park, from the dock at the foot of Brock Street, there are regular **cruises** ❷ out to and among the **Thousand Islands**, which speckle the St Lawrence River as it leaves Lake Ontario. Geologically, the Thousand Islands form part of the Frontenac axis, a ridge of million-year-old rock that stretches down into New York State. Indigenous peoples called the islands Manitouana – the "Garden of the Great Spirit" – in the

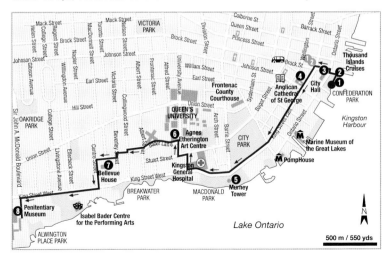

Thousand Islands

belief they were created when petals of heavenly flowers were scattered on the river; more prosaically, the islands later gave their name to a salad dressing. The Thousand Islands first hit the national headlines in the late 1830s, when they were the haunt of an irascible Canadian pirate, William Johnston, whose irritation with the British prompted him and his gang to spend several years harrying British shipping and Canadian farmers until he retired (with his booty) to New York State. Thereafter, the islands became a popular retreat for the rich and famous, including Irving Berlin and Jack Dempsey. The islands range from tiny hunks of rock that are bare and bleak to much larger islets with thick forest and lavish second homes, and although it's a pretty cruise at any time of the year, it's especially so in fall when the leaves turn. Several companies offer cruises from Kingston, but the benchmark is set by **Kingston 1000 Islands Cruises** (tel: 613-549-5544; www.1000islands cruises.ca; mid-May–mid-Oct 1–3 daily), whose three-hour sightseeing excursions are as good as any.

If you are feeling peckish after the cruise, wander up Princess Street to one of the city's most atmospheric restaurants, **Chez Piggy**, see ➊.

Just Room Enough Island, Thousand Islands

CITY HALL

Behind Confederation Park is **City Hall** ➌ (June–Sept regular guided tours: tel 613-546-0000; www.cityofkingston. ca), a copper-domed, stone extravagance which, with its imposing neoclassical columns and portico, dominates the waterfront as was intended – a suitably grand structure for what was scheduled to be the Canadian Parliament. By the time the building was completed in 1844, Kingston had lost its capital status and – faced with colossal bills – the city council had to make some quick adjustments, filling the empty corridors with shops and stalls and even a saloon. Things are more sedate today, with municipal offices occupying most of the space, but the guided tour does provide a fascinating insight into the

City Hall　　　　　　　　　　　　*Lock on the Rideau Canal*

development of the city and includes a trip up the clock tower.

ANGLICAN CATHEDRAL

It's a five-minute walk west from City Hall to Kingston's finest limestone building, the **Anglican Cathedral of St George** ❹ (tel: 613-548-4617; www.st georgescathedral.ca), at King and Johnson streets. Dating from the 1820s, the stirring lines of the cathedral, with its handsome portico and dainty domes, are deceptively uniform, for the church was remodeled on several occasions, notably after severe fire damage in 1899. The capacious interior holds some delightful Tiffany stained-glass windows and, attached to the wall of the nave, is a plain memorial to Molly Brant (1736–97), a Mohawk leader and sister of Joseph Brant. From the cathedral, it's a brief stroll to the main commercial drag, Princess Street, whose assorted shops, offices and cafés stretch up from the lakeshore.

MURNEY TOWER

From the the Anglican Cathedral, it's a 10-minute stroll west to **Murney Tower** ❺ (tel: 613-507-5181; mid-May–Aug daily 10am–5pm), by the lake at the foot of Barrie Street. The most impressive of four such towers built in Kingston to defend the dockyards against an anticipated US attack in the 1840s, this one is packed with military memo-

Kingston to Ottawa

If you're travelling on from Kingston to Ottawa, the obvious route is east along Hwy 401 and north up Hwy 416. With more time, take Hwy 15 and, at **Smiths Falls**, Hwy 43 (and ultimately hwys 2, 5, 13 and 73) inland from Kingston as these roads follow much of the route of the Rideau Canal (boats mid-May to mid-Oct; www.pc.gc.ca). Completed in 1832 the 202-km canal and its 24 lock stations cuts through the coniferous and deciduous forest, bogs, limestone plains and granite ridges separating Ottawa and Kingston. It was intended to provide inland transport at a time of poor Anglo-American relations, but after the political situation improved it developed as a route for regional commerce. The canal's construction led to the development of Bytown, renamed Ottawa in 1855, but in the nineteenth century the railways made it obsolete. The two most interesting are **Kingston Mills** (Locks 46–49), 12km inland from Kingston on Hwy 15, and **Jones Falls** (Locks 39–42), about 50km from Kingston with the complex including four locks, a dam and more.

To break the journey, visit **Merrickville** (Locks 21–23), 100km or so from Kingston. It takes five days (and lots of cash) to get from Kingston to Ottawa by boat on the Rideau Canal with Ontario Waterways (tel: 1-800-561-5767, http://ontariowater waycruises.com); there are between three and six cruises monthly from mid-May to mid-October; reservations are essential.

Historical European paintings at the Agnes Etherington Art Centre

rabilia including old weapons, uniforms and re-created nineteenth-century living quarters. The design of the tower, built as a combined barracks, battery and storehouse, was copied from a Corsican tower (at Martello Point) that had proved particularly troublesome to the British navy. A self-contained, semi-self-suffi-cient defensive structure with thick walls and a protected entrance, the Martello design proved so successful that tow-ers like this were built throughout the empire, only becoming obsolete in the 1870s with advances in artillery tech-nology. Incidentally, on Christmas Day 1885, members of the Royal Canadian Rifles regiment set out to skid around the frozen lake equipped with their field hockey sticks and a lacrosse ball, thereby inventing – or at least so King-stonians assert – the sport that has become a national passion/obsession.

THE AGNES ETHERINGTON ART CENTRE

Striking out west along King Street and then north along Lower University Ave-nue, it takes about 10 minutes to reach the first-rate **Agnes Etherington Art Centre** ❻ (tel: 613-533-2190; www. agnes.queensu.ca; Tue–Fri 10am–4.30pm, Sat–Sun 1–5pm), in the midst of the Queen's University campus, whose various college buildings fan out in all directions. The gallery has an excellent reputation for its temporary exhibitions, so the paintings are regularly rotated,

but the first two rooms usually kick off in dramatic style with a vivid selection of Canadian Abstract paintings. Beyond, a healthy slice of gallery space is devoted to the Group of Seven, while Tom Thom-son chips in with his studied *Autumn, Algonquin Park*. Other interesting exhibits to look out for are the Inuit prints of Keno-juak and Pitseolak. They are two of the best-known Inuit artists of modern times.

BELLEVUE HOUSE

Proceeding west along Bader Lane from the Agnes Etherington Art Centre, it's an easy 1km (0.6 mile) ramble to the intriguing **Bellevue House** ❼ (tel: 613-

Bellevue House

Penitentiary Museum

545-8666; www.pc.gc.ca; Apr–May & Sept–Oct daily 10am–5pm; June–Aug daily 9am–6pm), at 35 Centre Street. In the 1840s, Sir John Alexander Macdonald (1815–91), a leading politician and two-time prime minister, rented the house, a bizarrely asymmetrical, pagoda-shaped building, which he had taken a real shine to. The idea also was that the country air would improve the health of Macdonald's wife, Isabella, whose tuberculosis was made worse by the treatment – laudanum. Isabella never returned to good health and died after years as an invalid, leaving Macdonald alone (with the bottle). Both the house and gardens have been restored to the period of the late 1840s, when the Macdonalds lived here.

THE PENITENTIARY MUSEUM

From Bellevue House, it's another 1km (0.6 miles) west along King Street West to the intriguing **Penitentiary Museum** ❽ (tel: 613-530-3122; www.penitentiarymuseum.ca), which occupies the former prison warden's house dating from the 1870s – today's penitentiary is just across the street. The house was built by the prisoners and seven of its rooms now hold a fascinating assortment of exhibits, from examples of inmate arts and crafts to contraband the prisoners smuggled in and escape devices by which means they intended to get out – and no wonder they did: the "Punishment and Restraint" section has examples of the

sort of fate awaiting them, from a simple wooden easel to which prisoners were tied for a flogging through to the large and cumbersome contraption for a touch of water-boarding.

Doubling back along the lakeshore from the Penitentiary Museum, it takes about 40 minutes to stroll over to the first-rate **Le Chien Noir Bistro** for dinner and drinks, see ❷.

Food and Drink

❶ CHEZ PIGGY

68 Princess Street tel: 613-549-7673, www.chezpiggy.com; daily L and D; $$
Something of a Kingston institution, where locals bring their kith and kin to celebrate, this large, split-level restaurant is housed in restored stables dating from 1810. The patio is packed in summer and the attractive interior has kept its rough stone walls. The wide-ranging menu features all manner of main courses served in bountiful helpings, from Thai and Vietnamese through to South American and standard North American dishes.

❷ LE CHIEN NOIR BISTRO

69 Brock Street tel: 613-549-5635, www.lechiennoir.com; daily L and D; $$$
Spirited bar-cum-bistro with smart, modern decor and a first-rate menu featuring local, seasonal ingredients in creative combinations; try the free-range chicken with cheddar grits and asparagus.

Parliament Buildings

OTTAWA HIGHLIGHTS

The proud capital of Canada, Ottawa is a lively cosmopolitan city of around one million inhabitants, and its attractions include a clutch of outstanding national museums, a pleasant riverside setting, a busy café–bar and restaurant scene and superb cultural facilities. Be sure to visit.

DISTANCE: 10km (6 miles) partly walking, partly by bus
TIME: Two days
START: Parliament Hill
END: Laurier House
POINTS TO NOTE: Ottawa's most central sights are readily explored on foot, but a couple of the more outlying attractions are better reached by bus. City-wide bus services are provided by OC Transpo (tel: 613 741 4390; www.octranspo.com).

Almost all of Ottawa's major sights are clustered on or near the south bank of the Ottawa River to either side of the **Rideau Canal**. It's here you'll find the monumental Victorian architecture of **Parliament Hill**, the outstanding art collection of the **National Gallery of Canada**, and the **Byward Market**, the hub of the restaurant and bar scene. Many visitors only cover these, but there are a clutch of other attractions, most memorably the fascinating **Canadian War Museum**, housed in a strik-

ing building a couple of kilometres to the west of the centre, and **Laurier House**, packed with the possessions of the former Prime Minister William Lyon Mackenzie King and located 1.5km southeast of downtown.

PARLIAMENT HILL

Perched high above the Ottawa River, on the limestone bluff that is **Parliament Hill**, Canada's postcard-pretty **Parliament Buildings ❶**, (tel: 613-992-4793; www.parl.gc.ca) have a distinctly ecclesiastical air, their spires, pointed windows and soaring clock tower amounting to "a stupendous splodge of Victoriana" as one travel writer expressed it. Begun in 1859 and seventy years in the making, the complex comprises a trio of sturdy neo-Gothic structures, whose architectural certainties were both a statement of intent for the emergent country and a demonstration of the long reach of the British Empire. The Parliament Buildings were designed to be both imperial and imperious, but they certainly didn't

Library of Parliament

overawe the original workmen, who urinated on the copper roof to speed up its oxidization.

Allow a couple of hours to visit Parliament Hill – including Centre Block (see below) – a little longer if you want to witness the popular **Changing of the Guard**, when the Governor General's Foot Guards march onto Parliament Hill dressed in full ceremonial uniform of bright-red tunics and bearskin helmets (for times, see website).

CENTRE BLOCK

Dominating architectural proceedings on Parliament Hill is **Centre Block** ❷ (guided tours only; for details see website), home of the Senate and the House of Commons and in fact a replacement for the original building, which was destroyed by fire in 1916. This second structure was supposed to be the same as its predecessor, but it ended up about twice the size. The **Peace Tower**, rising from the middle of the facade, was added in 1927 as a tribute to Canadians who served in World War I. The tower can be visited on a self-guided tour (see website), but not on the guided tour, whose (changeable) itinerary includes a quick gambol round the **House of Commons**, where the Speaker's chair is partly made of English oak from Nelson's flagship *Victory*, and the red-carpeted **Senate**, which, with its murals of scenes from World War I, is surmounted by a beautiful gilded ceiling. At the back of the Centre Block is the **Library**, the only part of the building to have survived the fire of 1916; the circular design and the intricately carved wooden galleries make it parliament's most charming space.

The **debates** in both the House of Commons and the Senate are open to the public, who can observe proceedings from the public galleries. Most of the gallery seats are pre-booked, but a small number are allocated on the day, on a first-come, first-served basis: ask for further information on arrival. To check what is being debated and when, consult the website. Parliament's liveliest debates are usually during **Question Period**, when the Opposition interrogates the prime minister.

CONFEDERATION SQUARE

Triangular **Confederation Square**, ❸, a five-minute stroll from Parliament Hill, is a breezy open space dominated by the magnificent **National War Memorial**, in which a soaring stone arch is surmounted by representations of Liberty and Peace. Down below, a swirling, finely executed bronze depicts returning service men and women passing through the arch – from war to peace – and manages to convey both their exultation and sorrow. On the southeast side of the square is the complex of low concrete buildings that houses the **National Arts Centre** (see

Lock on the Rideau Canal

page 121), which clunks down to the Rideau Canal.

THE RIDEAU CANAL

From the National Arts Centre, take the old towpath along the **Rideau Canal** ❹, and, in a couple of minutes, you'll reach the long and extraordinarily pretty flight of **locks**, which step down to the Ottawa River with Parliament Hill rising on one side, the Fairmont Château Laurier hotel on the other. In winter, it's perhaps even better as this narrow sliver of water becomes the world's longest skating rink. Beside the foot of the locks is the **Bytown Museum** ❺ (www.bytown museum.com), Ottawa's oldest building, where military supplies were stored during the construction of the canal. Here,

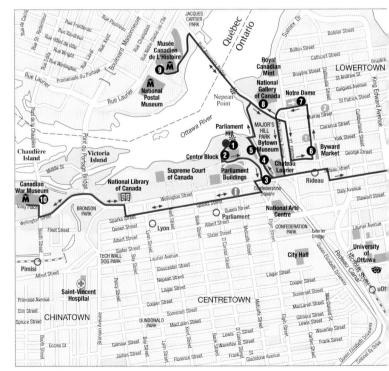

Boating down the canal   *Notre Dame cathedral*

a short film explores the history of the waterway and the difficulties involved in its construction; afterwards you can take a peek at a scattering of bygones from the city's earliest days. Incidentally, from mid-May to early October, **canal boat trips** leave from the top of the locks, and **river trips** from the bottom about five times daily; for further details, go to www.ottawaboatcruise.com.

BYWARD MARKET

Now is a good time for a break and fortunately the legion cafés and restaurants in and around the **Byward Market** ❻ are near at hand: from the Bytown Museum, cross the canal and walk round the northern edge of Major's Hill Park before looping back down Sussex Drive, a total distance of about 1km (0.6 miles); one good place to head for is **French Baker**, see ❶, a couple of blocks from the market, the second is **Zak's Diner**, see ❷.

NOTRE DAME

Strolling north from the Byward Market, through one of Ottawa's liveliest neighbourhoods, it's approximately 800m (0.5 miles) to the capital's Catholic cathedral, **Notre Dame** ❼ (tel: 613-241-7496; www.notredameottawa.com), whose twin silver spires poke high into the sky. Completed in 1890, this neo-Gothic cathedral has a nave that reaches a sort of ecclesiastical crescendo in a massive high-altar piece, flanked by a herd of pious wooden sculptures, many of which were carved by the carpenters and masons who worked on the Parliament Buildings. It's a fantastic place to visit in the city.

NATIONAL GALLERY OF CANADA

Across the street from Notre Dame, the **National Gallery of Canada** ❽

Interior of Byward Market

(tel: 613-990-1985; www.gallery.ca) occupies a cleverly conceived modern building whose acres of glass reflect the turrets and pinnacles of Parliament Hill. The collection was founded in 1880 by the then-governor general, who persuaded each member of the Royal Canadian Academy to donate a paint-

Byward Market

Since the 1840s, **Byward Market** (known simply as "The Market" to locals), just east of Sussex Drive and north of Rideau Street, has been a centre for the sale of farm produce, but it's now also Ottawa's busiest district, buzzing until the early hours. At its heart, the 1920s **Byward Market building** (Mon–Wed, Thu 9.30am–8pm, Fri & Sat 9.30am–6pm, Sun 9.30am–5pm; www.byward-market.com) is home to cafés and delis, specialist food and fresh fruit and vegetable stalls and these merge with the street stalls and kiosks outside. These stalls and kiosks are something of an Ottawa institution, mainly on account of their poutine (fries covered in gravy and cheese curds), but **Beavertails**, at the junction of George and William streets, weighs in with its eponymous offering, a flat, deep-fried dough sprinkled with all sorts of sweet toppings. Look for the Savour Ottawa (www.savourottawa.ca) logo as you're shopping – this indicates food that's grown or raised in and around Ottawa.

ing or two. Over the next century artworks were gathered from all over the world, resulting in a permanent collection now numbering more than 25,000 pieces. There's not enough space for all the paintings to be exhibited at any one time, so works from the collection are regularly rotated, and the gallery also offers world-class temporary exhibitions; free plans of the gallery are issued at reception.

The **Canadian galleries** are the finest, following the history of Canadian painting from the mid-eighteenth century to modern times. Nineteenth-century highlights include a good sample of the work of Cornelius Krieghoff, who could turn his hand to anything requested by his middle-class patrons; the unique Croscup Room, once the ornate living room of a Nova Scotian shipping family; and the evocative frontier scenes of Paul Kane, Canada's first artist-explorer. In the first half of the twentieth century, it was the **Group of Seven** who developed a Canadian aesthetic in a style of paintings that aimed to capture the spirit and vastness of the northern landscape. The several rooms devoted to the Group's canvases feature the seminal paintings of both Tom Thomson and Lawren Harris. More modern works include a stirring selection of abstract paintings produced in Montréal from the 1940s to the 1970s and a section devoted to American Abstract Expressionists. The gallery also boasts a small but eclectic collection of Inuit

National Gallery of Canada

art and sculptures. The kernel of the material is its soapstone sculptures, but there are whale bone and ivory pieces, as well as brightly coloured drawings.

MUSÉE CANADIEN DE L'HISTOIRE

Just a few metres from the National Gallery of Canada, the Alexandra Bridge offers great views, but lots of traffic, as it spans the Ottawa River to reach **Gatineau**, a predominantly francophone settlement now firmly incorporated within the Capital Region. It takes about 10 minutes to walk over the bridge to get to Gatineau's pride and joy, the **Musée Canadien de L'Histoire ❾** (Canadian Museum of History; tel: 819-776-7000; www.historymuseum.ca), whose distinctive, curvy limestone contours are supposed to represent the rocky sweep of the Canadian Shield. The museum focuses on Canada's turbulent history with separate sections on, for example, Early Canada, Colonial Canada and Modern Canada. Perhaps the highlight, however, is the **Grand Hall**, easily the largest room in the museum and perfectly designed to display a magnificent collection of around twenty Pacific Coast totem poles. The main line of poles stands outside six Indigenous "houses" which explore Pacific Coast culture, including displays on trade, religious beliefs, tribal gatherings and art.

As you might expect, the museum has a couple of cafés and a bistro – but frankly you're better off catching the bus back to the city centre and returning to the Byward Market area, where there are lots of places to eat and drink (see page 82); buses leave from outside the museum every few minutes. Now might also be a good time to settle down in your hotel (see page 106), leaving the remaining two major sights – the Canadian War Museum (see below) and Laurier House (see page 84) – until the morning.

CANADIAN WAR MUSEUM

Start your morning at Confederation Square (see page 79), from where pedestrianized Sparks Street leads west on the first part of the 2km-long (1.2 miles) ramble – or quick bus ride –

The Grand Hall, Canadian Museum of History

Canadian War Museum

over to the **Canadian War Museum ⑩** (tel: 819-776-7000; www.warmuseum. ca), which is housed in a striking modern building beside the Ottawa River. This exemplary museum is divided into several distinct display areas, which work their way through Canada's military history with accompanying text and quotations. The first gallery, the "Battleground: Wars on Our Soil, earliest times to 1885", features a good selection of Native Canadian weaponry – tomahawks, muskets and so forth – plus a particularly well-researched section on the War of 1812. However, the museum really gets into its stride when it reaches **World War I**. There are lots of fascinating photographs, but it's the incidental detail that impresses most:

Canada was keen for its soldiers to use a Canadian rifle, but the end product – the Ross Rifle – often jammed, while the rum ration came in barrels labelled "SRD" (Service Regimental Depot), which the troops rebranded as "Seldom Reaches Destination". The section on World War II is similarly intriguing and there's good stuff on the Cold War too – including details of the strange case of the Russian defector Igor Gouzenko, who was so scared of retribution that he was often interviewed with a bag over his head. Finally, the **Lebreton Gallery** is a large hangar packed with all sorts of military hardware, such as tanks, armoured cars and artillery.

After your visit, its easy to catch the bus back to the city centre with some services continuing on to Laurier House (see below).

Laurier House

LAURIER HOUSE

Celebrated as one of Ottawa's most intriguing historical attractions, **Laurier House ⑪** (tel: 613-992-8142; www.pc.gc.ca), is located some 1.7km (1 mile) southeast of Confederation Square on Laurier Avenue East. The house was the home of two former prime ministers, Sir Wilfred Laurier, Canada's first French-speaking prime minister, who served from 1896 to 1911, and William Lyon Mackenzie King, his self-proclaimed "spiritual son" and Canada's longest serving PM – from 1921 to 1930 and 1935 to 1948. Notoriously

Algonquin Provincial Park

pragmatic, King enveloped his listeners in a fog of words through which his political intentions were barely discernible. The perfect illustration – and his most famous line – was "not necessarily conscription, but conscription if necessary", supposedly a clarification of his plans at the onset of World War II. Even more famous than his obfuscating rhetoric was his personal eccentricity. His fear that future generations would view him negatively led him into spiritualism. He held regular séances to tap the advice of great dead Canadians, including Laurier, who allegedly communicated to him through his pet dog.

King's possessions dominate the house; look for his crystal ball and a portrait of his obsessively adored mother, in front of which he placed a red rose every day. The house also contains a reconstruction of a study belonging to another prime minister, **Lester B. Pearson**, who was awarded the Nobel Peace Prize for his role in resolving the Suez Crisis. Pearson also had a stab at devising a new flag for his country and, although it was rejected, the mock-up he commissioned, with blue stripes at either end to symbolize the oceans, is on display here.

THE WILDERNESS: ALGONQUIN PROVINCIAL PARK

If you hanker for the great Canadian wilderness, you might consider driving to **Algonquin Provincial Park** (www. algonquinpark.on.ca), just 245km (152 miles) west of Ottawa. This great slab of untamed parkland boasts dense hardwood and pine forests, canyons, rapids, scores of lakes and, amongst a rich wildlife, loons, beavers, moose, timber wolves and black bears. Canoeing and hiking are the big deals here, and several companies offer all-inclusive wilderness packages, including meals, permits, guides, equipment and transport to and from the park. One of the best companies is **Call of the Wild** (tel: 905-471-9453; www.callofthewild.ca), which runs a varied programme that includes three-day and five-day canoeing trips deep into the park.

Food and Drink

❶ THE FRENCH BAKER

119 Murray Street; tel: 613-789-7941; www.frenchbaker.ca; daily B and L; $
Much-lauded bakery, with a handful of seats for in-house eating, that does a great line in French bread and sells what many local thinks are the best croissants in town.

❷ ZAK'S DINER

14 Byward Market Square; tel: 613-241-2401; www.zaksdiner.com; open 24hr, seven days a week; $
A 1950s-style time warp with chrome decor, rock 'n' roll blaring from the jukebox and all-American food – stick to the shakes and the burgers.

Hikers in Georgian Bay Islands National Park

SEVERN SOUND AND GEORGIAN BAY

If you're eager to escape the bustle of Toronto, a top choice is to head north to Severn Sound, whose deep-blue waters are studded by rocky islets. There are two historical sites hereabouts too – Discovery Harbour and Sainte-Marie among the Hurons.

DISTANCE: 60km (38 miles) from Penetanguishene to Honey Harbour via Discovery Harbour. Or 410km (255 miles) beginning and ending in Toronto.
TIME: Two days
START: Penetanguishene
END: Beausoleil
POINTS TO NOTE: It's not possible to complete this route by public transport – you will need your own vehicle. The route described begins in Penetanguishene, which is 165km (102 miles) from downtown Toronto, a little under 2 hours' drive north of the city along Hwy 400. It includes a boat trip to and from Beausoleil Island, so you should check sailing times (and make a reservation) before you depart. Also note that if you intend to go hiking on the island, you should come properly equipped. Without the boat trip, this route can be done in a day – but it would be quite a slog.

The southern shore of **Severn Sound**, a little under 2 hours' drive from Toronto, is one of the most delightful parts of Ontario, its creeks and bays dotted with tiny ports, its waters sprinkled with thousands of islets. It's here you'll find two of the province's most important historical reconstructions – **Discovery Harbour**, a British naval base, and **Sainte-Marie among the Hurons**, a Jesuit mission. Be sure to spare some time for the wonderful scenery of the **Georgian Bay Islands National Park**, whose glacier-smoothed, Precambrian rocks and wispy pines were so marvellously celebrated by Canada's own Group of Seven painters.

PENETANGUISHENE

A convenient place to start this tour is homely **Penetanguishene** ❶ ("place of the rolling white sands" in Ojibwa), the westernmost town on Severn Sound and just 165km (102 miles) from downtown Toronto. The town's Main Street is a pleasant place for a stroll, its shops installed behind old and sturdy redbrick facades, which slope down towards the waterfront and the intriguing Centennial Museum, at 13 Burke Street and Beck Boulevard (tel: 705-549 2150;

HMS Tecumseth at Discovery Harbour

www.pencenmuseum.com; July–Aug daily 9am–4.30pm, Sept–June Tue–Fri 9am–4.30pm, Sat 9am–12.30pm & 1–4.30pm). The museum occupies the old general store and offices of the Beck lumber company, whose yards once stretched right along the harbour. The company was founded in 1865 by Charles Beck, a German immigrant who made himself immensely unpopular by paying his men half their wages in tokens that were only redeemable at his stores. The museum has several displays on the Beck lumber company, including examples of these "Beck dollars", and there's also a fascinating selection of old photographs featuring locals at work and play in the town and its forested surroundings.

Penetanguishene was the site of one of Ontario's first European settlements – a Jesuit mission founded in 1639 and then abandoned a decade later following the burning of Sainte-Marie (see page 88). Europeans returned some 150 years later to establish a trading station, but the settlement remained insignificant until the British established a naval dockyard here (see page 88) following the Anglo-USA War of 1812. This attracted both French- and English-speaking shopkeepers and suppliers, and even today Penetanguishene is one of the few places in southern Ontario to maintain a bilingual tradition.

If you are feeling peckish, pop into one of the diners on the Main Street such as **Phil's Family Restaurant**, see ❶.

DISCOVERY HARBOUR

Heading out of Penetanguishene, it's a signed 5km (3 miles) drive north along the bay to **Discovery Harbour** ❷ (tel: 705-549-8064; www.discoveryharbour. on.ca; late May–June Mon–Fri 10am–5pm, July–Aug daily 10am–5pm), an ambitious reconstruction of the naval base built here by the British in 1817. The primary purpose of the base was to keep an eye on American movements on the Great Lakes, and between 1820 and 1834 up to twenty Royal Navy vessels were stationed here. Ships from the base also supplied the British outposts further to

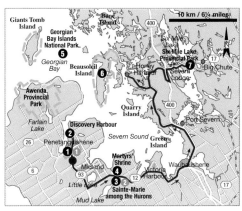

Sainte-Marie among the Hurons

the west and, to make navigation safer, the Admiralty decided to chart the Great Lakes. This monumental task fell to the base's Lieutenant Henry Bayfield, who informed his superiors of his determination "to render this work so correct that it shall not be easy to render it more so". He was as good as his word, but the naval station was more short-lived. By 1834, relations with the US were sufficiently cordial for the navy to withdraw, and the base was turned over to the army, who maintained a small garrison here until 1856. Today, staffed by enthusiastic costumed guides, the sprawling site spreads along a hillside above a tranquil inlet, its green slopes scattered with accurate reconstructions of everything from a sailors' barracks to several period houses, the prettiest of which is the Keating House, named after the base's longest-serving adjutant, Frank Keating. Only one of the original buildings survives, the dour limestone Officers' Quarters, which dates from the 1840s, but the complex's pride and joy is the working harbour-cum-dockyard, home to a a brace of fully rigged sailing ships, the HMS *Bee* and HMS *Tecumseth*.

SAINTE-MARIE AMONG THE HURONS

Proceeding southeast from Discovery Harbour, it's a signed 14km (8.7 mile) drive to Ontario's most arresting historical attraction, the reconstructed Jesuit mission of **Sainte-Marie among the Hurons** ❸ (tel: 705-526-7838; www. saintemarieamongthehurons.on.ca; early May and late Oct Mon–Fri 10am–5pm; late May–mid-Oct daily 10am–5pm), which marks the site of a crucial episode in Canadian history. In 1611, the French explorer Samuel de Champlain formed an alliance with the Huron of southwest Ontario, but his gift of firearms disrupted the balance of power among the native societies of the St Lawrence and Great Lakes areas. Armed with Champlain's rifles, the Huron attacked their ancient enemies, the Iroquois, who vowed revenge.

Meanwhile, in 1639, the Jesuits had established their centre of operations at Sainte-Marie. Here, they converted Indigenous to Christianity, but much more importantly they had unwittingly infected the Huron with three European sicknesses: measles, smallpox and influenza; the results were well-nigh cataclysmic.

Ten years later, the Iroquois, now armed with Dutch muskets, invaded Huron territory – Huronia – slaughtering their enemies as they moved in on Sainte-Marie. Fearing for their lives, the Jesuits of Sainte-Marie burned their settlement and fled. Eight thousand Hurons went with them and most starved to death on the islands of Georgian Bay and a handful of Jesuits were slain, too.

A visit to Sainte-Marie starts in the reception centre with a film show that provides background information before the screen lifts dramatically away to reveal the painstakingly restored mis-

Martyrs' Shrine

sion site. There are 25 wooden buildings here, divided into two sections: the Jesuit area with its watchtowers, chapel, forge, living quarters, well-stocked garden and farm buildings, complete with pigs, cows and hens; and the native area, including a hospital and a pair of bark-covered long houses – one for Christian converts, the other for non-Christians. Fairly spick-and-span today, it takes some imagination to see the long houses as they appeared to Father Lalemant, who saw "…a miniature picture of hell… on every side naked bodies, black and half-roasted, mingled pell-mell with the dogs… you will not reach the end of the cabin before you are completely befouled with soot, filth and dirt".

Costumed guides act out the parts of Hurons and Europeans with great gusto, answering questions and demonstrating crafts and skills, though they show a certain reluctance to eat the staple food of the region, sagamite, a porridge of cornmeal seasoned with rotten fish. The grave in the simple wooden **church of St Joseph** between the Christian and native areas is the place where the (remaining) flesh of two of the murdered monks, Brébeuf and Lalemant, was interred after the Jesuits had removed the bones for future use as reliquaries.

A path leads from the site to the excellent museum, which traces the story of the early exploration of Canada with maps and displays on such subjects as fishing and the fur trade, seen in the context of contemporary European history. This leads into a section on the history of the missionaries in New France, with particular reference to Sainte-Marie. Information on the archaeology of the site follows: the mission's whereabouts were always known even though Victorian settlers helped themselves to every chunk of stone – from what was known locally as "the old Catholic fort" – because the Jesuits had deposited the necessary documentation in Rome. Excavations began on the site in the 1940s and continues today.

Allow at least a couple of hours to explore the site and afterwards take lunch at the popular **Restaurant Sainte-Marie**, see ②.

THE MARTYRS' SHRINE

Overlooking Highway 12 immediately to the west of the entrance to Sainte-Marie Among the Hurons is the **Martyrs' Shrine** ④ (tel: 705-526-3788; www.martyrs-shrine.com; mid-May–mid-Oct daily 9am–9pm), a twin-spired, 1920s church perched on a wooded hill. The church commemorates the eight Jesuits who were killed in Huronia between 1642 and 1649. Blessed by Pope John Paul II in 1984, the church, along with the assorted shrines and altars in its grounds, is massively popular with pilgrims. Inside, the transepts hold a number of saintly reliquaries, most notably a stack of crutches discarded by healed pilgrims and the skull of the monk Brébeuf, who fled Ste-Marie only to be captured by the Iroquois nearby.

Beausoleil Island

GEORGIAN BAY ISLANDS NATIONAL PARK

The pint-sized port and hamlet of **Honey Harbour**, 36km (23 miles) north of Sainte-Marie, is the handiest base for exploring the **Georgian Bay Islands National Park ⑤**, which comprises a scattering of about 60 islands spread between Severn Sound and Twelve Mile Bay, approximately 50km to the north. The park's two distinct landscapes – the glacier-scraped rock of the Canadian Shield and the hardwood forests and thicker soils of the south – meet at the northern end of the largest and most scenic island, **Beausoleil ⑥**. This island is a 15-minute boat ride west of Honey Harbour with the national park's **Georgian Bay Islands Day Tripper boat** (tel: 877-737-3783; www.pc.gc.ca/en/pn-np/on/georg/visit/daytripper), which departs three times daily from mid-May to early October with around 4 hours' hiking time allowed on the island. Reservations are required and double check return ferry times before you disembark. Prospective hikers need to come equipped – this is a wilderness environment.

Beausoleil has 11 short **hiking trails**, including two that start at the Cedar Spring landing stage on the southeastern shore: Treasure Trail (3.8km), which heads north behind the marshes along the edge of the island, and the Christian Trail (1.5km), which cuts through beech and maple stands to balsam and hemlock groves overlooking the rocky beaches of the western shoreline. At the northern end of Beausoleil, the Cambrian (2km) and Fairy trails (2.5km) are routes through harsher glacier-scraped scenery, while, to the west, the Dossyonshing Trail (2.5km) tracks through an area of wetland, forest and bare granite that covers the transitional zone between the two main landscapes.

After, you'll be in Honey Harbour; the best accommodation around is at **Severn Lodge ⑦**, a 30-minute drive east from Honey Harbour along country roads.

Food and Drink

① PHIL'S FAMILY RESTAURANT
48 Main Street, Penetanguishene; tel: 705-549-7858; www.philspenetang.com; daily B, L, and D; $
Friendly and agreeable diner offering a straightforward Canadian menu at very affordable prices – think steak, spaghetti, fish and chips and the like. Enjoy a range of assorted pies and cakes for dessert. Check out the daily specials, too.

② RESTAURANT SAINTE-MARIE
16164 ON-12, Midland; tel: 705-526-7838; www.saintemarieamongthehurons. on.ca; daily B and L; $
The restaurant at Sainte-Marie may lack a little atmosphere, but the food is tasty, comprising a good selection of traditional Canadian cuisine with a few 'pioneer/ historical' surprises.

Lake Huron shore near Pinery Provincial Park

SOUTHWEST ONTARIO: LAKE HURON AND STRATFORD

There's something to cater for most tastes on this varied route – from scenic sunsets over Lake Huron and Goderich's charming Victorian buildings through to the small-town charms of leafy Bayfield and the theatrical delights of Stratford. Unmissable.

DISTANCE: 335km (209 miles)
TIME: Two to three days
START: Goderich
END: Stratford
POINTS TO NOTE: It's a 3-hour drive west from Toronto to the Lake Huron shoreline at Goderich, the starting point for this driving tour. You will need your own vehicle – public transport, where it exists at all, is thin on the ground. The best places to stay are in Bayfield (see page 107) and Stratford (see page 107).

Heading west from Toronto, you eventually escape the city's sprawling suburbs and satellite townships to emerge in **rural Ontario**, a sprawling chunk of flat and fertile farmland that extends as far as the shores of Lake Huron. Famous for its sunsets – and much less polluted than Lake Ontario – the Huron lakeshore is trimmed by sandy beaches and a steep bluff, which is interrupted by the occasional river valley. The first targets here are **Goderich**, with its cluster of historic buildings, and lovely **Bayfield**, arguably the prettiest town in Ontario. From here, you can nudge south to investigate the assorted sites associated with the early oil boom – the **Oil Museum** is intriguing – then loop down to **Uncle Tom's Cabin Historic Site**, a reminder of the cruel days of slavery. From here, you can cut back towards Toronto, stopping at Stratford, much celebrated for its outstanding Shakespeare Festival.

GODERICH

Nudging the Lake Huron shoreline, **Goderich** ❶ is a delightful, laidback country town of eight thousand inhabitants, which dates back to the 1820s. Begin this walking tour right in the middle of town, on **Courthouse Square**, a neat and trim, geometrically planned central circus, which is dominated by a handsome, white stone courthouse. From here, a set of four wide, tree-lined avenues radiate out, each following the points of the compass. Proceed along North Street and it's about

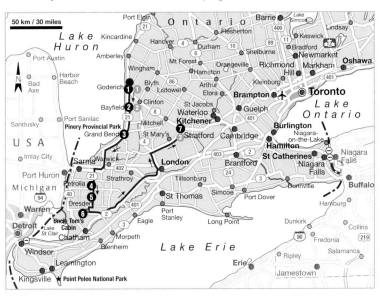

Goderich's beach and salt works

300m (330 yards) to the compendious **Huron County Museum** (tel: 519-524-2686; www.huroncountymuseum.ca; Jan−Apr Mon−Fri 10am−4.30pm and Sat 1−4.30pm; May−Dec Mon−Sat 10am−4.30pm and Sun 1−4.30pm), which concentrates on the exploits of the district's pioneers. Highlights include a fantastic array of farm implements, from simple hand tools to gigantic, clumsy machines like a steam-driven thresher. There's also a beautifully restored Canadian Pacific steam engine, as well as exhibition areas featuring pioneer furniture and military memorabilia.

HURON COUNTY GAOL

From the Huron County Museum, it's a 10-minute walk to the high stone walls of the **Huron County Gaol**, at 181 Victoria St (tel: 519-524-6971; www.huroncountymuseum.ca; mid-May−early Sept daily 10am−4.30pm): to get there, walk up to the far end of North Street, then turn right along Gloucester Terrace and it's at the end of the street on the right. This joint courthouse and jail was constructed between 1839 and 1842, but the design was very unpopular with local judges, who felt threatened by the

Victorian architecture in Goderich

proximity of those they were sentencing. The other problem was the smell: several judges refused to conduct proceedings because of the terrible odour coming from the privies in the exercise yard below and, in 1856, the administration gave in and built the new courthouse that now stands in the central circus. On a visit to the gaol, don't miss the original jailer's apartment and a string of well-preserved prison cells, which reflect various changes in design between 1841 and 1972, when the prison was finally closed. The worst is the leg-iron cell for "troublesome" prisoners, where unfortunates were chained to the wall with neither bed nor blanket.

WEST STREET AND THE LAKESHORE

Returning the way you came, it's an easy 1km (0.6 miles) stroll from the County Gaol back to Courthouse Square, where you can stop for lunch at one of several family-run diners such as **West Street Willy's Eatery**, see ⓘ. To extend your explorations thereafter, leave Courthouse Square along **West Street**, which leads the 1km (0.6 miles) through a cutting in the bluffs to the harbour and salt workings on the **Lake Huron shoreline**. From here, a footpath (2.5km/1.5miles) trails north round the harbourside silos to the **Menesetung Bridge**, a former railway crossing that now serves as a pedestrian walkway spanning the Maitland River. On the far side of the river, you can pick up the **Maitland Trail**, which wanders down the north bank of the river as far as the marina. In the opposite direction from the end of West Street, the shoreline has been tidied up to create a picnic area, but, although the sunsets are spectacular, the beach itself is a tad scrawny.

BAYFIELD

Pocket-sized **Bayfield** ❷, just 20km south of Goderich, is an extraordinarily pretty and prosperous little town with handsome timber villas nestling beneath a canopy of ancient trees. The townsfolk have kept modern development at arm's length – there's barely a neon sign in sight, never mind a concrete apartment block – and almost every house has been beautifully maintained. Stroll along Bayfield's short **Main Street**, examining the historical plaques that give the low-down on the older buildings, and in a few minutes you'll reach pint-sized **Pioneer Park**, on the bluff overlooking the lake – and a fine spot to take in the sunset. Bayfield is mainly a place to relax and unwind, but you can also venture down to the **harbour** on the north side of the village, where, in season, you can pick wild mushrooms and fiddleheads along the banks of the Bayfield River; allow a couple of hours for this excursion. Bayfield is a lovely

Sunset at Pinery Provincial Park

place to spend the night and cream of the hotel crop is the **Little Inn of Bay-field** (see page 107); the food is outstanding there, too, see ➋.

PINERY PROVINCIAL PARK

Begin the morning with a leisurely breakfast in Bayfield before driving the 40km (25 miles) south along the Lake Huron shoreline to the **Pinery Provincial Park** ➌ (tel: 1-888-668-7275; www.ontarioparks.com/park/pinery). It would be easy to spend the whole day here as the park has lots to offer – from hiking trails that weave through dunes and woodland to freshwater canoeing and paddle boarding – but most visitors opt for a laze on the sandy beach. If you are keen to see more of the area, limit yourself to a couple of hours here before moving on.

PETROLIA

Leaving Pinery Provincial Park, push on south along the lakeshore before branching off onto Highway 30 to reach, after 60km (37 miles), the tiny but intriguing township of **Petrolia** ➍. Here, the grand stone-and-brick buildings that distinguish the town centre speak volumes about the sudden rush of wealth that followed the discovery of the oil in the late nineteenth century. The first prospectors were attracted to the area by the patches of black and sticky oil that had seeped to the surface through narrow fissures in the rock. In 1858 James Miller Williams dug North America's first commercial oil well hereabouts, and in 1862 a certain Hugh Shaw drilled deeper than anyone else and, at 49 metres, struck the first gusher. The shock of seeing the oil fly up into the trees prompted Shaw, a religious man, to use the words of his Bible – "And the rock poured me out rivers of oil" (Job 29:6).

At the height of the boom, the Ontario oilfields produced about 30,000 barrels of crude a day and as the proceeds rolled in, Petrolia's Victorian mansions and expansive public buildings followed. Several of these handsome historic buildings have survived, dotted along and around the main drag, **Petrolia Line**, and are viewable on a brief – say 15-minute – drive around town. Three prime examples are the **Municipal Offices**, at Petrolia Line and Greenfield Street; **Nemo Hall**, an impressive brick building decorated by splendid wrought-iron trimmings at 419 King St and Victoria Street; and **St Andrew's Presbyterian church**, close by at Petrolia Line and Queen Street, which is awash with neo-Gothic gables and towers. To emphasize the town's origins, its streetlamps are cast in the shape of oil derricks, but once you've admired the architecture there is no particularly strong reason to hang around – and you can then press on south to Oil Springs.

The Henson homestead, Uncle Tom's Cabin Historic Site

OIL SPRINGS

Heading south from Petrolia, it's just 13km (8 miles) to **Oil Springs** ❺, which is home to the intriguing **Oil Museum of Canada** (tel: 519-834-2840; www.lambtonmuseums.ca; May–Oct daily 10am–5pm; Nov–Apr Mon–Fri 10am–5pm), which has been built next to the site of James Williams' original oil well. Highlights of the open-air display area include a nineteenth-century blacksmith's shop, with some fascinating old sepia photos taken during the oil boom and an area of gum bed. The inside of the museum has a motley collection of oil-industry artefacts and background geological information. Oil is still produced in the fields around the museum. It is drawn to the surface and pushed on into an underground system of pipes by some seven hundred low-lying pump jacks, which once formed the nucleus of a rough-and-ready frontier district whose flat fields were packed with hundreds of eager oil-seekers and their hangers-on.

UNCLE TOM'S CABIN

From Oil Springs, it's a 28km (17 miles) drive to the agricultural town of Dresden, on whose outskirts is **Uncle Tom's Cabin Historic Site** ❻ (tel: 519-683-2978; www.uncle tomscabin.org; late May–June and Sept–late Oct Tue–Sat 10am–4pm, Sun noon–4pm; July & Aug daily 10am–4pm), comprising a handful of old wooden buildings, most notably a plain and simple church. Here also is the clapboard house that was once the home of the Reverend Josiah

> ## Underground Railroad
>
> The **Underground Railroad (UGRR)** started in the 1820s as a loose and secretive association of abolitionists dedicated to smuggling slaves from the southern states of America to Canada. By the 1840s, the UGRR had become a well-organized network of routes and safe houses, but its real importance lay not so much in the number of slaves rescued – the total was small – but rather in the psychological effect it had on those involved in the smuggling. The movement of a runaway usually involved very few people, but many more, particularly neighbours and friends, knew what was happening and therefore were complicit in the breaking of the law. To the extent that white Americans could be persuaded to accept even the most minor role in the UGRR, the inclination to compromise with institutional slavery was undermined, though the psychology of racism remained intact: like Beecher Stowe's Uncle Tom, the freed were supposed to be humble and grateful, simulating childlike responses to please their white parent-protectors.

Avon River, Stratford

Henson, a slave who fled from Maryland to Canada in 1830 by means of the Underground Railroad, or UGRR (see page 95). Henson and a group of abolitionist sympathizers subsequently bought 200 acres of farmland here round Dresden and founded a vocational school for runaway slaves. Unable to write, Henson dictated his life experiences and in 1849 these narrations were published as *The Life of Josiah Henson – Formerly a Slave*. It's a powerful tract, unassuming and almost matter of fact in the way it describes the routine savagery of slavery – and it was immediately popular. One of its readers was **Harriet Beecher Stowe**, who met Henson and went on to write the most influential abolitionist text of the day, *Uncle Tom's Cabin* (1852), basing her main character on Henson's accounts. Most of the Dresden refugees returned to the US after the Civil War, but Henson stayed on, accumulating imperial honours that must have surprised him greatly – he was even presented to Queen Victoria; he died in 1883. Henson's book is quite difficult to get hold of, but copies are sold here and there is also a small museum on slavery plus an intriguing video giving more details and information on Henson's life and times.

It is advised to allow an hour or so for your visit; if you are feeling like having something to eat, you might choose to grab a bite in Dresden, but you may want to wait as there is a far better range of places in Stratford such as the Italian/Mediterranean restaurant, **Fellini's**, see ❸. It is a 2-hour drive away and the final port of call on this particular route.

The Stratford Festival

Each year, North America's largest classical repertory company puts on the **Stratford Festival** (tel: 519-273-1600 or 1-800-567-1600; www.stratfordfestival.ca), featuring two of Shakespeare's tragedies and one of his comedies; this programme is augmented by other classical staples – Molière, Chekhov, Jonson and so forth – as well as by the best of modern and musical theatre. The festival also hosts a lecture series, various tours (of backstage and a costume warehouse, for example), music concerts, an author reading series and meet-and-greet sessions with the actors. The festival runs from mid-April to late October and there are performances in four downtown theatres – the Festival, the Tom Patterson, the Avon and the Studio. Regular **tickets** cost between $50 and $100 depending on the performance and seat category, though there are all sorts of discount deals for students, seniors, same-day performances and previews; many plays are sold out months in advance. Call or check the website to book.

Stratford City Hall

STRATFORD

From Uncle Tom's Cabin, it is a 2-hour drive northeast (160km/100 miles) to **Stratford** ❼, a likeable town comprised of 30,000 people, which rises head and shoulders above its neighbours as the host of the impressive **Stratford Festival** (see page 96). Originating in 1953, Stratford Festival is now one of the most prestigious theatrical occasions in North America, attracting no fewer than half a million visitors every year. It only takes an hour or so to work out what is where in Stratford, beginning with the town's downtown core, on and around the intersection of Ontario and Downie streets. Here a handsome set of nineteenth-century brick facades reaches an idiosyncratic hiatus in the grandiose **city hall**, a brown-brick confection of cupolas, towers and limestone trimmings. In addition, the town is bisected by the meandering **Avon River**, whose leafy banks are lined with immaculately maintained footpaths and overlooked by the largest of the town's four theatres, the **Festival Theatre**. As you might well expect for such a popular tourist destination, Stratford has an extensive range of first-rate B&BS (see page 107) to stay in and the city offers several excellent restaurants (see page 115) to dine in, too. Travellers are well-catered for in this area, making a visit to the city of Stratford even more enjoyable.

Food and Drink

❶ WEST STREET WILLY'S EATERY
42 West Street, Goderich;
tel: 519-524-7777; www.weststreetwillys eatery.com; Wed–Sun 8am–8pm; B, L, and D; $
Friendly, small-town diner in neat and trim premises near the Courthouse Square. Serves up filling portions of well-prepared home-made stalwarts – burgers and soups, of course, but also tacos and a tasty fisherman's chowder.

❷ LITTLE INN OF BAYFIELD
26 Main Street North, Bayfield; tel: 519-565-2611 or 1-800/565-1832; www.littleinn.com; daily 8am–9.30pm; B, L, and D; $$$
This delightful hotel, in a creatively updated, early nineteenth-century timber-and-brick building, has a smart and chic restaurant. The menu is varied and usually includes freshwater fish from Lake Huron – perch, white fish, pickerel or steelhead.

❸ FELLINI'S
107 Ontario Street; tel: 519 271 3333; www.fellinisstratford.com; daily L and D; $$
This large Italian/Mediterranean restaurant with garish but somehow rather cheery decor serves up a compelling range of pizzas and pasta dishes. It has a handy, central location, too.

DIRECTORY

Hand-picked hotels and restaurants to suit all budgets and tastes, organized by area, plus select nightlife listings and an overview of the best books and films to give you a flavour of the region.

The Anndore House

ACCOMMODATION

As you might expect of a major metropolis, **Toronto** offers a wide range of accommodation with something to suit every budget, though prices rise steeply at the most popular times of the year. The middle section of the market is dominated by the high-rise **hotels** that are liberally dotted around Downtown. Most of them are operated by the larger chains, which means you can guarantee comfort, if not especially style, though this changes as the price goes up – the most expensive chain hotels are lavish indeed. Rather more interesting are the quirky **boutique hotels** that have shaken up the city's hotel scene in the last twenty years – **The Drake Hotel** (see page 104) and **The Gladstone Hotel** (see page 104) come to mind. At the least expensive end of the market, you can count on **motels** as providing reliable accommodation, though to get to many of them you will need a car, and then there are the **bed & breakfast** places – some simple and plain, others ornate and fanciful.

Outside of Toronto, the small towns of **Ontario** can usually muster an inexpensive motel or two and there is a scattering of deluxe resorts amongst the more visited lakes. **Ottawa**, on the other hand, weighs in with a string of chi-chi hotels and **Kingston** is known for its vintage B&Bs.

Wherever you are staying, you can anticipate complimentary WiFi, but breakfasts are generally not included in the room rate and neither is parking in the big cities, notably Toronto and Ottawa. Reservations are well-nigh essential in the busy summer months. All hotels, motels, and resorts accept major credit cards, and all are completely smoke-free. Although the price ranges we have quoted are for the lowest rack rate at the time of going to press, ask about special packages and promotions when making a reservation.

Price for a standard double room for one night, excluding taxes and breakfast, in high season.

$$$$ = over $400
$$$ = $250–400
$$ = $150–250
$ = less than $150

Toronto's City Centre

The Anndore House
15 Charles Street East; tel: 416-924-1222; www.theanndorehouse.com; $$$
Industrial with an Art Deco vibe, this 11-storey brick boutique hotel features rooms that resemble a hip designer's space with exposed brick walls, leather chairs, subway-tiled bathrooms and vinyl record players. The lovely hotel restaurant, Constantine, has a

Lovely touches at The Ivy at Verity

Mediterranean-focused menu that can be enjoyed all day, notably for brunch.

Bisha Hotel Toronto

80 Blue Jays Way; tel: 1-866-497-1788; www.bishahoteltoronto.com; $$$

At the epicentre of the Entertainment District, this chic and lush hotel is filled with art and even has an entire floor designed by rocker Lenny Kravitz. The rooftop patio and outdoor infinity pool have stunning views of Downtown.

Chelsea Hotel

33 Gerrard Street West; tel: 416-595-1975; www.chelseatoronto.com; $$

This is Canada's largest hotel, a smart and modern place with a very family-friendly vibe, including a special KidZone, two indoor swimming pools, an indoor water slide, and several eateries to choose from. The Family Fun Suites come with an Xbox and other toys.

Courtyard by Marriott Toronto Downtown

475 Yonge Street; tel: 416-924-0611; www.marriott.com; $$

Neat and trim and good value, this modern, centrally located hotel keeps it simple and practical. Some rooms have balconies with city views, and the fitness centre is open 24hrs.

Fairmont Royal York

100 Front Street West; tel: 416-368-2511; www.fairmont.com; $$$

In a prime location, opposite Union Station, this historic, château-style, landmark hotel comes complete with a fabulous lobby of mosaic floors, coffered ceilings and extravagant chandeliers. The rooms beyond are not quite as grand, but they are very comfortable with all mod cons.

Hilton Toronto

145 Richmond Street West; tel: 416-869-3456; www.hilton.com; $$

This large business hotel offers comfortable, well-appointed rooms in classic chain style. The hotel also has a capacious heated indoor/outdoor pool with a bar, and the suites are suitable for extended stays.

HI Toronto

76 Church Street; tel: 416-971-4440; www.hihostels.ca; $

Lively hostel with simple shared rooms or private rooms with en-suite bathrooms. A breakfast voucher is included and can be used at the onsite Cavern Bar, which gets busy in the evenings so the hostel also provides free earplugs. Barbecues are held on the rooftop patio, weather permitting.

The Ivy at Verity

111 Queen Street East; tel: 416-368-6006; www.theivyatverity.com; $$$$

Toronto's classiest hotel, this chi-chi boutique hotel is located in a restored Victorian chocolate factory and features just four exquisitely decorated rooms with private terraces. Continen-

The Consort Bar at The Omni King Edward Hotel

tal breakfast is included and delivered right to your room.

The Omni King Edward Hotel
37 King Street East; tel: 416-863-9700; www.omnihotels.com; $$$
Built in 1903, the King Edward has a grand and imposing facade and, although the interior is not quite as well preserved, it does have its stylistic moments – as do the well-appointed guest rooms.

One King West Hotel & Residence
1 King Street West; tel: 416-548-8100; www.onekingwest.com; $$$
Upscale and notably grand hotel converted from the historic 19th-century Toronto Dominion Bank building, with much of the structure's original character still preserved. The rooms are contemporary, however, and have well-appointed kitchenettes.

Planet Traveler Hostel
357 College Street; tel: 647-352-8747; www.theplanettraveler.com; $
Inside a restored historic brick building, this appealing hostel has a choice of basic shared dorm-style or private rooms. A free and unlimited breakfast is included, and the rooftop patio with its solar-panelled roof has great city skyline views. Closed at the time of writing, but should reopen in due course.

The Ritz-Carlton
181 Wellington Street West; tel: 416-585-2500; www.ritzcarlton.com; $$$$
Expect high-end, spacious rooms with impressive marble bathrooms complete with TVs in the mirrors, plus heated floors, at this large Ritz hotel. The full-service spa and Italian restaurant are excellent as well.

St Regis Hotel
325 Bay Street; tel: 416-306-5800; www.marriott.com; $$$
Chic hotel in the centre of it all, with suites that include gas fireplaces, wet bars, and soaker tubs. The heated indoor saltwater pool on the 32nd floor has wide views of the Toronto skyline.

A Seaton Dream B&B
243 Seaton Street; tel: 416-929-3363; www.aseatondream.com; $$
A welcoming bed & breakfast in a Victorian-era townhouse. There are three, en-suite guest rooms here with fine traditional decor, including hardwood floors. A hot breakfast and parking are included.

Shangri-La Hotel Toronto
188 University Avenue; tel: 647-788-8888; www.shangri-la.com; $$$$
Luxury high-rise hotel located right in the Financial District, featuring elegant Asian-inspired decor and a huge, 24-hour fitness centre that includes a yoga studio. The vibrant lobby has live music most evenings.

SoHo Metropolitan
318 Wellington Street West; tel: 416-599-

The indoor pool at the St Regis Hotel

8800; www.sohohotel.ca; $$$
Popular with visiting celebrities, this relaxed, boutique hotel has a complimentary luxury sedan service and an upscale all-day dim sum eatery. The top-notch fitness centre even comes with a personal trainer. Pricey and luxurious.

Windsor Arms Hotel
18 St Thomas Street; tel: 416-971-9666; www.windsorarmshotel.com; $$$$
Opulent vintage hotel from the 1920s with period decor and modern amenities such as Nespresso machines. The suites even include a musical instrument to use. The indoor saltwater pool is lovely, and the location is in Toronto's prime shopping district, Bloor-Yorkville.

Toronto's Midtown
Four Seasons Hotel Toronto
60 Yorkville Avenue; tel: 416-964-0411; www.fourseasons.com; $$$$
One of the city's best hotels, offering the epitome of modern luxury. Guest rooms are bright and feature signature Four Seasons beds with down duvets and pillows. There's a top-ranking on-site restaurant, an exquisite spa, and an ultra-modern fitness centre with a yoga studio and pool.

The Hazelton Hotel
118 Yorkville Avenue; tel: 416-963-6300; www.thehazeltonhotel.com; $$$$
Luxurious and pet-friendly boutique property with spacious guest rooms that include heated granite floors and rainfall showers. The indoor saltwater pool is small but amazing, and the classy lobby bar serves up fabulous cocktails.

Kimpton Saint George
280 Bloor Street West; tel: 416-968-0010; www.kimptonsaintgeorge.com; $$$
A luxury boutique hotel featuring a vintage colour palette and modern furnishings. Rooms come with record players and yoga mats. Complimentary bikes are available, too, plus there's a wine hour each evening, a 24-hour fitness centre, and a lively gastropub onsite.

Yorkville Royal Sonesta Hotel
220 Bloor Street West; tel: 416-960-5200; www.sonesta.com; $$
Routine, modern high-rise holding a smart and very comfortable hotel with a good range of facilities. Popular with visiting business folk. The hotel also boasts a pleasant courtyard patio for the warmer months.

Toronto's Eastside
The Broadview
106 Broadview Avenue; tel: 416-362-8439; www.thebroadviewhotel.ca; $$$
With roots dating back to 1891, this historic building in the up-and-coming Leslieville neighbourhood has left its seedy past well behind – it was the location of a strip club – and is now a luxury boutique hotel with beautiful, individually unique rooms. It also boasts a fabulous rooftop bar and restaurant.

Room at The Westin Harbour Castle Hotel

Toronto's Westside

1hotel
550 Wellington Street West; tel: 406-640-7778; www.1hotels.com/toronto; $$$
Chic and hip boutique hotel featuring gorgeous, modern rooms with luxurious marble bathrooms. Check out the lively rooftop bar and infinity pool with amazing city and lake vistas and excellent cocktails.

Annex Garden Bed & Breakfast
445 Euclid Avenue; tel: 416-258-1179; www.annexgarden.com; $$
Charming B&B in the Little Italy neighbourhood, on a former estate from 1885. The Victorian and Edwardian architectural features of the house have been carefully restored, and modern amenities have been added. Rooms and suites are luxurious with fireplaces and en-suite bathrooms; rates include breakfast and parking.

By The Park Bed & Breakfast
92 Indian Grove; tel: 416-520-6102; www.bythepark.ca; $$
Well-established, spotless, and sophisticated bed & breakfast consisting of two heritage houses. One has four suites – and rates include a vegetarian breakfast – the other offers five self-catering suites. All suites include parking, some have fireplaces and full kitchens.

The Drake Hotel
1150 Queen Street West; tel: 416-531-5042; www.thedrake.ca; $$$
Popular, fashionable and artsy boutique hotel in the Arts and Design District. Guest rooms are colourful, contemporary and unique. With multiple restaurants and bars onsite, there's always an event happening here, from an art show to live music.

Gladstone Hotel
1214 Queen Street West; tel: 416-531-4635; www.gladstonehotel.com; $$
Housed in a Victorian brick building, this charming, art-focused boutique hotel has around forty unique, artist-designed guest rooms to choose from. Perks include free bike loans, yoga classes and frequent art exhibits.

Old Mill Toronto
9 Old Mill Road, Etobicoke; tel: 416-232-3703; www.oldmilltoronto.com; $$
For a romantic getaway just outside of downtown, this elegant Tudor-style property right along the Humber River is just perfect. The spacious rooms include four-poster beds, Jacuzzi tubs, and stunning views of the lush grounds and surrounding river valley.

Toronto's Waterfront

Radisson Blu Toronto Downtown
249 Queen's Quay West; tel: 1-437-886-9667; www.radisson.com; $$
Modern and stylish, harbourfront hotel, a quick streetcar ride from Downtown. The best rooms have panoramic CN Tower and lake views, and some even have gas fireplaces. The large outdoor

Cadillac Motel, straight out of a movie

pool and patio are lively during the summer months.

The Westin Harbour Castle Hotel
1 Harbour Square; tel: 416-869-1600; www.marriott.com; $$$

Twin 34-story waterfront towers make up this urban modern resort, complete with a large fitness centre, an indoor pool, tennis courts, full service spa, and various eateries to choose from. It's also family and pet friendly, with special amenities and services for both.

Best Western Plus Travel Hotel Toronto Airport
5503 Eglinton Avenue West, Etobicoke; tel: 416-620-1234; www.bestwestern. com; $

A practical option for staying close to the Toronto Pearson International Airport, this business hotel has clean, comfortable rooms, a small fitness center, a complimentary airport shuttle, and a complimentary breakfast.

Homewood Suites by Hilton Toronto Airport Corporate Centre
5515 Eglinton Avenue West, Etobicoke; tel: 416-646-4600; www.hilton.com; $$

Convenient airport location for short and long-term stays, with large, modern suites that include a fully equipped kitchen. Other extras include an onsite 24-hour convenience store, fitness centre, indoor pool, and a courtyard with a barbecue area and putting green.

Cadillac Motel
5342 Ferry Street, Niagara Falls; tel: 905-356-0830; www.cadillacmotelniagara. com; $

Built in 1957, this well-known, garish-meets-kitsch motel has featured in quite a few Hollywood movies. Today, the modest and trendy retro-style rooms include private bathrooms, a mini-fridge, air conditioning and free parking. The falls are just two blocks away.

Sterling Inn & Spa
5195 Magdalen Street, Niagara Falls; tel: 289-292-0000; www.sterlingniagara.com; $$

The spacious rooms of this modern hotel boast four-poster beds, hardwood floors, fireplaces and steam-shower bathrooms. A tasty continental breakfast is delivered to your room each morning. The onsite AG restaurant (see page 115) is a real highlight.

Abacot Hall Bed & Breakfast
508 Mississauga Street, Niagara-on-the-Lake; tel: 905-468-8383; www.abacothall. com; $$

Well-run, friendly bed & breakfast in an elegant, Georgian-style home surrounded by manicured gardens. Each of the en-suite rooms has been beautifully decorated and has air conditioning. There's also a delightful cook-to-order breakfast.

A suite at the Queen's Landing

The Butler House Historic Bed & Breakfast

67 Mary Street, Niagara-on-the-Lake; tel: 905-468-8985; www.thebutlerhouse.ca; $$
Romantic bed & breakfast with an English country charm set in a property dating back to 1814. Rooms are beautifully decorated and feature all modern facilities. Breakfast is a gourmet, three-course banquet.

Queen's Landing

155 Byron Street, Niagara-on-the-Lake; tel: 905-468-2195; www.vintage-hotels.com; $$$
This Georgian-style stately hotel was actually built in 1990 on the site of the Old Niagara Harbour and Dock Company building from 1831. There are four special Dockmasters Suites that are located in the historic annex of the dock company and are true pinnacles of luxury.

Kingston

Hochelaga Inn

24 Sydenham Street South; tel: 613-549-5534; www.thehochelagainn.ca; $$
This sprawling inn, located in a residential area within easy walking distance of the centre, occupies a good-looking Victorian mansion with a playful central tower, bay windows and wraparound verandah. There are around twenty guest rooms, all en-suite, and each is very comfortable.

Rosemount Inn

46 Sydenham Street South; tel: 613-480-6624; www.rosemountinn.com; $$
An eminently appealing B&B, which occupies a strikingly handsome, distinctively Italianate old limestone villa – one of Kingston's finest buildings. The Rosemount has ten guest rooms, all en-suite, decorated in attractive period style. The breakfasts are delicious, too.

Secret Garden Inn

73 Sydenham Street South; tel: 613-548-1081; www.thesecretgardeninn.com; $$
One of Kingston's most enjoyable inns, with seven extremely comfortable rooms, all en-suite and each decorated in charming antique style. The house is a fetching Victorian building of timber and brick with verandahs and porches and a splendid bay-windowed tower.

Ottawa

Andaz Ottawa Byward Market

325 Dalhousie Street; tel: 613-321-1234; www.hyatt.com; $$
This sleek hotel covers most items on a top hotel checklist: great location, style and amenities. The rooms are elegant with natural colours and wide views through the windows. The rooftop lounge is the highest bar in town, with stunning vistas and an expert cocktail menu.

Fairmont Château Laurier

1 Rideau Street; tel: 613-241-1414; www.fairmont.com; $$$
The Grand Trunk Pacific Railway built this prestige hotel in the 1910s and it remains Ottawa's finest, comprising a wonderful example of the French

Room with a view at the Andaz Ottawa Byward Market

Renaissance – or château – style: the exterior is a forest of copper-clad turrets, spires and towers, and inside the public areas boast marble floors, high ceilings, chandeliers and soaring columns, plus extravagantly embossed elevators. The guest rooms are thoroughly comfortable, done up in a muted palette of creams and browns, and the best offer delightful views toward the Ottawa River. Discounts are legion.

McGee's Inn

185 Daly Avenue; tel: 613-237-6089 or 1-800-262-4337; www.mcgeesinn.com; $

On a leafy side-street a short walk from downtown, McGee's occupies a grand old Victorian redbrick. The interior is decorated in attractive period style and the guest rooms are charming, a nice mix of the old and the new. The two best rooms have their own balcony. Breakfasts are first rate – and home cooked.

Port Severn

Severn Lodge

116 Gloucester Trail; tel: 705-756-2722 or 1-800-461-5817; www.severnlodge.com; $$$

This luxurious lodge has a wonderful solitary location amid a dense forest overlooking a wide and quiet section of the Trent–Severn Waterway. The main lodge and chalets have all the facilities of a mini-resort, including canoe and motorboat rental, an artificial beach, a restaurant and an outdoor swimming pool. To get there, leave Hwy-400 at Exit 162 – and the lodge is 7km along Route 34. Minimum two-night stay in the summer; price includes meals.

Bayfield

Little Inn of Bayfield

26 Main Street North; tel: 519-565-2611 or 1-800-565-1832; www.littleinn.com; $$

The best hotel for miles around, the Little Inn occupies a tastefully modernized early nineteenth-century timber-and-brick building with a handsome second-floor verandah and delightfully furnished rooms, mostly with Jacuzzis; there's an annexe across the street with equally pleasant rooms, too.

Stratford

Acrylic Dreams B&B

66 Bay Street; tel: 519-271-7874; www.acrylicdreams.com; $$

Handily located a 10min walk from the main crossroads, this cottage-style timber house, which dates from the 1870s, has four intimate guest rooms decorated in pastel browns and creams. The owners serve up home-made breakfasts with the vegetarian in mind.

Stone Maiden Inn

123 Church Street; tel: 519-271-7129; www.stonemaideninn.com; $$

Immaculately maintained 1873 Victorian house with a variety of guest rooms of varying size and luxury, though all have period trimmings. Complimentary coffee and tea. Good location too, a short walk south of the main crossroads.

The open kitchen at Buca

RESTAURANTS

Every inch a cosmopolitan city, Toronto boasts a wonderfully varied and exciting army of cafés and restaurants with something for every palate and every would-be gastronome. There is something for every size of pocketbook, too, from the smart and the chic restaurant, where you'll surrender a fair wad of cash, to hole-in-the-wall places where a few dollars will suffice. One thing that strikes the visitor is the passion with which locals embrace their food, a passion which is quite enough to sustain some seven thousand restaurants spread right across the city. All this choice also means that competition is fierce, so both the service and quality of the food are almost always good, often excellent.

Here in Toronto, flavours are truly global: you can sample authentic Chinese dim sum, enjoy first-rate Italian pizzas and try Vietnamese street food – all within easy striking distance of each other. Indeed, sometimes the sheer variety can be a bit overwhelming,

though you can, if struck by indecision, always resort to simple sandwiches and salads, which are widely available at scores of cafés. Alternatively, one pleasant way to sample the menu – and enjoy the ambience – of a pricier establishment is to take advantage of a lunch menu; these tend to be much better value than dinner menus.

Restaurant opening hours and times of peak flow vary, so it's a good idea to make a reservation, but more so in the evening than at lunch time; whatever the time of day, a 15–20 percent tip is customary if the service was good. For an up-to-the-minute scoop on who the best chefs are and where to dine, consult the glossy **Toronto Life** (www.torontolife.com) magazine, which publishes regular reviews and news.

City Centre

Aloette

163 Spadina Avenue; tel: 416-260-3444; www.aloetterestaurant.com; daily L and D; $$$

Sleek and elegant French bistro with a diner feel, located on the ground level of the same building as its fine-dining sister Alo, upstairs. The menu is simple but special with a fantastic beef carpaccio, and a notable house burger. Aloette doesn't take reservations, so come early.

Price for a two-course meal for one including a glass of wine (or other beverage).
$$$$ = over $60
$$$ = $45–60
$$ = $20-–45
$ = under $20

Burger and fries at Chubby's Jamaican Kitchen

Beast Bodega

96 Tecumseth Street; tel: 647-352-6000; www.beastbodega.ambassador.ai; Wed–Sun L and D; $$

Tucked away on a quiet residential street, Beast is considered a meat-focused restaurant, but it's really all about the biscuits (buns) here – specifically, the biscuit sandwiches. House-made, buttermilk-rich, and super soft and flaky, at brunch time they can be filled with a choice of eggs, fried chicken, peameal bacon, smoked brisket, or even just served with a luscious gravy.

Buca

604 King Street West; tel: 416-865-1600; www.buca.ca; daily D; $$$

Rustic Italian fare, including house-made charcuterie, fresh pastas and pizzas, served super efficiently. If you're looking for more of a cocktail and shared plates kind of spot, head over to the equally great Bar Buca, just a block south at 75 Portland St.

Byblos

11 Duncan Street; tel: 647-660-0909; www.byblostoronto.com; daily D; $$$

Saffron, anise, za'atar, and other exotic spices and fragrances of Eastern Mediterranean cuisine come alive here, with a choice of a bright and airy main floor for seating or a more sultry lounge upstairs. To start, try the duck kibbeh appetizer, followed by the short rib kebab, a fatoush salad, and, to finish, the orange blossom mousse.

Bymark

66 Wellington Street West; tel: 416-777-1144; www.mcewangroup.ca; Mon–Fri L and D, Sat D; $$$$

There's much more to this suit and tie restaurant than the famous, and also amazing, $40 burger, even if it comes served with shaved truffles and brie cheese. The new Canadian cuisine crafted and presented here is utterly fantastic. Try their take on the classic poutine – with butter-braised lobster.

Chubby's Jamaican Kitchen

104 Portland Street; tel: 416-792-8105; www.chubbysjamaican.com; daily L and D; $$

Be transported to the Caribbean, with a retro-resort decor, papaya salads, sizzling meats on the grill, and cocktails served inside pineapples. Finish the meal in style with a passion fruit coconut cream pie.

Jacobs & Co. Steakhouse

12 Brant Street; tel: 416-366-0200; www.jacobssteakhouse.com; daily D; $$$$

An elegant steakhouse for those special (carnivorous) occasions, with white linens, first-rate service, and even a piano bar. Caesar salad is prepared table side, the steak menu is according to its origin, from local to Japanese beef, and the wine list is extensive.

King's Noodle Restaurant

296 Spadina Avenue; tel: 416-598-1817; daily B, L and D; $

Traditional Chinatown restaurant complete with roasted duck and pork hanging

in the window. Don't expect stellar service, but do expect delicious barbecued duck, fried dough fritters and fresh noodle dishes. This is a cash-only establishment.

Kinka Izakaya Original

398 Church Street; tel: 416-977-0999; www.kinka.com; daily L and D; $$
Boisterous Japanese pub with delicious small plates to share and lots of drinks to choose from. This is a perfect spot for an adventurous group looking to try some unusual dishes – or opt for the set menu to play it (relatively) safe.

Kojin

190 University Avenue; Third Floor; tel: 647-253-8000; www.kojin.momofuku.com; Mon–Fri L; daily D; $$$
Part of the international Momofuku restaurant brand, this stunning Canadian cuisine-focused restaurant harnesses the best local produce, seafood, and meats available, and uses a wood-fire grill for much of the cooking.

Kupfert & Kim

140 Spadina Avenue; tel: 416-502-2206; www.kupfertandkim.com; daily B, L and D; $$
'Wheatless and meatless' is the proud slogan of this small local fast-food chain. But don't think this translates as tasteless – this little take-out spot is excellent; everything is made in-house using mostly organic, local ingredients. The cauliflower tahini bowl is a must-try, with quinoa, hummus, a za'atar salsa and fresh veggies.

Mira

420A Wellington Street West; tel: 647-951-3331; www.mirarestaurant.com; daily D; $$
Colourful and contemporary Peruvian restaurant and bar with small plates of traditional and fusion bites such as yuca fries, beef tartare and lobster-topped rice. For dessert, the El Huevo Malo – essentially a giant chocolate Easter egg surprise, is unmissable.

Pearl Diver

100 Adelaide Street East; tel: 416-366-7827; www.pearldiver.to; Mon–Wed D, Thu–Sun L and D; $$
Relaxed seafood bar specializing in the freshest of oysters. Even better, perhaps, shrimp cocktails, chowders, and fish and chips are on the menu too. Try the 'Seafood Tower' for a bit of everything, and the summer takeout window is great for quick picnic orders.

Pow Wow Café

213 Augusta Avenue; tel: 416-551-7717; no website; daily L and D; $$
Tacos, Ojibwe-style, using frybread at this Indigenous Canadian-inspired eatery. There are usually four choices – beef chili, veggie chili, coconut lime chicken curry, and pork souvlaki. Each taco is generously portioned and delicious.

Rasa

196 Robert Street; tel: 647-350-8221; www.rasabar.ca; Mon–Sat D, Sun L; $$
Subterranean, industrial-chic space dishing up globally inspired and crea-

A tasty salad at Rasa

tively plated tapas such as empana-das, ceviche, steak tartare and roasted lamb. The cocktails are equally crea-tive – enjoy one or two outside in the heated, street-level patio.

Tinuno
31 Howard Street; tel: 647-343-9294; www.tinunothirtyone.com; daily B, L and D; $$
Bright and simple little place with mouthwatering traditional Filipino spe-cialties, all from the grill. Try the Kama-yan Feast, which is served on a banana leaf with sticky rice, and meant to be eaten with your hands. It includes an assortment of grilled seafood, meat and vegetables.

Midtown

Jacques Bistro du Parc
126A Cumberland Street; tel: 416-961-1893; www.jacquesbistro.com; Tue–Sat L and D; $$$
Locals have happily dined inside this sweet little French restaurant since the late 1970s – and luckily not a whole lot has changed since then. The refined menu is served in an unpretentious manner and offers classics such as onion soup, escargots, pâtés, mussels and specialty fresh fish dishes.

Planta
1221 Bay Street; tel: 647-812-1221; www.plantarestaurants.com; daily L and D; $$$
As the name suggests, all the dishes

served in this bright, modern vegan res-taurant are plant-based. And they are no ordinary dishes. Menu items include beautifully plated coconut ceviche, mat-cha soba noodles, tomato tarts, gour-met pizzas, and eggplant lasagne, to name but a few.

Pukka
778 St Clair Avenue West; tel: 416-342-1906; www.pukka.ca; daily D; $$$
Modern Indian restaurant with an excel-lent wine list. The menu offers sharea-ble and creative bar snacks, comforting curries using local ingredients such as wild sockeye salmon and Québec duck breast, and for dessert there's sticky toffee pudding and pavlova.

Westside

416 Snack Bar
181 Bathurst Street; tel: 416-364-9320; www.416snackbar.com; daily D; $$
Late-night casual eatery serving up an eclectic global menu of shareable small plates. The dishes are meant to reflect Toronto's diversity so expect Korean fried chicken, steamed pork buns, spicy tuna rolls, pakoras, falafel, oysters and more.

Bar Isabel
797 College Street; tel: 416-532-2222; www.barisabel.com; daily D; $$$
Lively and intimate Spanish tapas tav-ern with delicious small plates on offer for sharing, including cheeses, meats and seafood specialties. The cocktail

Simple but delicious fare awaits at Dandylion

and wine lists are excellent, too, and for a fee you can bring in your own bottle of wine if you wish.

Café Polonez

195 Roncesvalles Avenue; tel: 416-532-8432; www.cafepolonez.ca; daily L and D; $$

Rightfully located in the heart of the city's Polish community, this inviting, long time family-run restaurant serves up hearty portions of Eastern European favourites such as borscht, potato pancakes, goulash, pierogies, and schnitzel. There's a good selection of Polish beers and vodka as well.

Dandylion

1198 Queen Street West; tel: 647-464-9100; www.restaurantdandylion.com; Tue–Sat D; $$$

Cozy, narrow space with an exposed-brick decor and an open kitchen. The ever-changing and modest Canadian menu is unusual in that it only lists a handful of ingredients from each dish, so it's a bit of a surprise what arrives at the table, but always a delight.

Enoteca Sociale

1288 Dundas Street West; tel: 416-534-1200; www.sociale.ca; daily D; $$$

Quaint, rustic-looking and friendly trattoria serving fine cheeses, cured meats, house-made bread and fresh pastas. The wine list is fantastic, and there's even a real cheese cave in the basement.

Grand Electric

1330 Queen Street West; tel: 416-627-3459; www.grandelectrictoronto.com; daily L and D; $$

Local, vibrant, and loud hang-out for creative Mexican fare, such as tacos, quesadillas and tostadas, served at communal tables. Their unusual take on key lime pie is delicious.

Grey Gardens

199 Augusta Avenue; tel: 647-351-1552; www.greygardens.ca; daily D; $$$

Bright and breezy, with an open kitchen and a vintage feel, this place doubles as a terrific wine bar in the late evenings. Featuring an inventive North American menu – pick from vegetarian dishes, fresh seafood, steak, pasta and scrumptious desserts.

Hanmoto

2 Lakeview Avenue; Mon–Sat D; $$

Japanese dive bar with a kitchen that stays open till 2am offering a range of filling and superbly flavourful snack items. Try the decadent Katsu Bun, the Dyno wings (essentially stuffed chicken wings), or the Nasu Dengaku, a deep-fried eggplant dish with a miso hollandaise sauce and fried shredded beets.

La Banane

227 Ossington Avenue; tel: 416-551-6263; www.labanane.ca; daily D; $$$$

Modern French seafood bistro and bar with creative dishes on the menu, including the beautifully presented

Chefs at work at Grey Gardens

eurobass en croûte. For dessert, don't miss the Ziggy Stardust Disco Egg – a chocolate egg made with apricots, ancho chilies and coffee beans, and filled with chocolate truffles.

La Cubana

92 Ossington Avenue; tel: 416-537-0134; www.lacubana.ca; daily noon–10pm, Fri–Sat until midnight; $$

Fresh and cool lunchtime favourite on the Ossington Strip, featuring an amazing pressed Cubano sandwich made with thinly sliced ham, sous-vide pork shoulder, gruyère cheese, and some condiments. The Guava BBQ Short Rib is fantastic as well, with a side of Yuca Frita – crispy fried cassava root.

La Palma

849 Dundas Street West; tel: 416-368-4567; www.lapalma.ca; daily L and D, Sat–Sun B; $$$

Bright and airy northern Italian eatery and take-out counter with a beachy California vibe. Try the 100-layer lasagna with a perfect crust, the melt-in-your-mouth oxtail gnocchi, and for dessert, the sinful selection of donuts.

Mildred's Temple Kitchen

85 Hanna Avenue, Suite 104; tel: 416-588-5695; www.templekitchen.com; Sat–Sun B, daily L, Thu–Sat D; $$

A go-to spot for brunch on the weekends, this spacious and modern eatery is known city-wide for its stack of fluffy and thick blueberry-infused buttermilk pancakes. Not to miss either are the Huevos Monty with refried beans and spicy salsa or the big brunch skillet with pulled pork and potato hash.

Miss Thing's

1279 Queen Street West; tel: 416-516-8677; www.missthings.com; Tue–Sat D; $$

Hawaiian cocktail and snack bar with a beautiful, sophisticated tropical decor to match. The drinks are top-notch and fun. For food, try the pineapple jicama salad and the poke bowl.

Nuit Social

1168 Queen Street West; tel: 647-350-6848; www.nuitsocial.com; daily D; $$

A late night favourite for the bar crowd, or anyone up for a delicious nibble or two, this cosy hangout specializes in charcuterie boards. Build your own board from a list of locally sourced and fine imported meats, cheeses and olives, or pick from an Italian-inspired tapas menu.

Pinky's Ca Phe

53 Clinton Street; tel: 416-533-4488; Mon–Sat D; $$

Tucked away Vietnamese snack bar with an unassuming exterior, but the intimate and notably vintage decorated interior gives it an inviting and memorable atmosphere. Have a Foco Loco fruity cocktail with the full-flavoured tiger's milk ceviche, the marrow beef, and the lemongrass chicken banh mi sandwich.

Pizzeria Libretto

221 Ossington Avenue; tel: 416-532-8000; www.pizzerialibretto.com; daily L and D; $$

Possibly the best, most authentic Neapolitan-style pizza in town, with several Toronto locations. Their savoury pies are made with imported Italian ingredients and wood-fired in an oven made from Italian stones. The weekday lunch prix fixe deal is pretty good and includes a salad, pizza and dessert.

Rhum Corner

926 Dundas Street West; tel: 416-792-7511; www.rhumcorner.com; daily D; $$

Haitian watering hole, with simple, inexpensive, and also extremely tasty food and drinks. Go for the Pina Colada Slushie or Fresco cocktail, and share a few small plates of banana frites, salt cod patties and albacore tuna ceviche.

Simit & Chai Co.

787 King Street West; tel: 647-352-4161; www.simitandchai.co; daily B and L; $

Spacious, industrial yet cosy Turkish bakery specializing in simit, circular breads filled with savoury spreads like black olive paste or fava bean paste. Try them with Turkish coffee or tea.

Snakes & Lattes

600 Bloor Street West; tel: 647-342-9229; www.snakesandlattes.com; daily L and D; $

Pick a board game out of a collection of over 1,500, order some sandwiches and drinks, and get playing with your friends, or make new ones here at this concept café. The friendly staff can easily suggest a game and explain rules for any games that are unfamiliar.

Waterfront & Toronto Islands

Buster's Sea Cove

93 Front Street East (Upper Level of St Lawrence Market); tel: 416-369-9048; Tue–Sat B and L; $

One of the busiest stands at the St Lawrence Market, Buster's is all about fresh and local seafood. Choose from traditional fish and chips or go for the crab cake sandwich, but expect a line-up and there are only a few spots to sit down.

Churrasco's

93 Front Street East (Upper Level of St Lawrence Market); tel: 416-862-2867; www.stlawrencemarket.com; Tue–Sat B and L; $

Come here for the juiciest, most flavourful and tender rotisserie chicken basted in Churrasco's (secret) hot sauce. For dessert try their traditional Portuguese custard tarts – a sweet creamy egg custard filling inside a little, flaky pastry bowl.

European Delight

93 Front Street East (Lower Level of St Lawrence Market); tel: 416-365-9010; www.stlawrencemarket.com; Tue–Sat B and L; $

The specialty here is home-made Eastern European foods, such as Ukrainian pierogis, Hungarian blintzes, and Polish

cabbage rolls, plus borscht, latkes, and other delicious take-out options.

Niagara Falls

AG

5195 Magdalen Avenue, Niagara Falls; tel: 289-292-0005; www.agcuisine.com; Tue–Sun D; $$$

In amongst the neon lights and kitschy motels is this gem of a farm-to-table fine-dining establishment, located in the lower level of the Sterling Inn & Spa (see page 105). Much of the ingredients are grown on AG's own farm nearby, and all the wines are local. Try the grilled quail with a blueberry barley risotto, or the beef tenderloin with an almond brie crust.

Il Sorriso Café & Pizzeria

5983 Clark Avenue, Niagara Falls; tel: 905-353-1989; www.ilsorriso.ca; Thu–Sat L and daily D; $$

Welcoming family-run Italian pizza joint known for its stone-baked, thin-crust pizza with a huge choice of toppings to satisfy any palate. The generously filled calzones are just as tasty, and try the fun s'mores pizza for dessert.

Ottawa

Town

296 Elgin Street tel: 613-695-8696; www.towncitizen.ca; daily 5–11pm; $$

Feast on creative, artisanal Italian cuisine with a Canadian twist at this spirited restaurant. Start off with small bites like lavender almonds and fried Brussels sprouts with vegan cashew crema and then launch into main dishes, like ricotta-stuffed meatballs and pork cheek ragu.

Whalesbone Oyster Bar

430 Bank St at Gladstone; tel: 613-231-8569; www.thewhalesbone.com; daily L and D; $$

The best seafood joint in town, offering the freshest of fish in its antique, highly varnished premises. Famous for its oysters – but the other seafood dishes also impress, including the excellent shellfish risotto.

Stratford

Balzac's Coffee Roastery

149 Ontario Street; tel: 519-273-7909; www.shop.balzacs.com; $; daily B and L

This branch, the original of a medium-sized Ontario chain, sells a first-rate range of fair-trade coffees plus pastries and cakes. Prides itself on the quality of its coffee beans.

Sirkel Foods

40 Wellington Street; tel: 519-273-7084; www.sirklefoods.com; daily B and L; $

Kick off the day at this bustling café-restaurant across from Stratford's City Hall, which serves the heartiest breakfasts in town. Try the eggs Florentine or the lentil pancakes with salmon and sour cream. The sandwiches and salads are equally tasty, including the chicken pesto sandwich and the spinach salad with poached pears and blue cheese.

Outdoor tables at Bellwoods Brewery

NIGHTLIFE

Toronto's pulsating nightlife covers all the options – from swanky lounges and top-ranking dance clubs through to grungy basement hidey-holes and everything in between. Two particularly enticing areas, where Toronto is at its trendiest – in an avant garde sort of way – are the Ossington Strip and Queen Street West, though Little Italy, with some great cocktail bars, is not far behind. Live music is on offer in a hatful of places – Toronto has a strong reputation for jazz and blues – and the city also boasts world class theatre, both classical and contemporary. Toronto also possesses a platoon of cinemas, which is hardly surprising given that the city hosts one of the world's most acclaimed film festivals – the Toronto International Film Festival (www.tiff.net).

Toronto bars

BarChef

472 Queen Street West; tel: 416-868-4800; www.barcheftoronto.com

For a cocktail lounge, Gothic-like BarChef is the best, featuring the top mixologists in the city, who are busy creating amazing drinks accompanied by an easy-going soundtrack. Try the bay leaf and elderflower spritz or the vanilla hickory smoked Manhattan.

Bellwoods Brewery

124 Ossington Avenue; tel: 416-535-4586;
www.bellwoodsbrewery.com

Bright and industrial, this brewpub has a comfortable cottage-like decor. There's an excellent selection of house-brewed beer and accompanying bites to eat. The outdoor patio out front is one of the best spots for a drink when the weather is cooperating.

Birreria Volo

612 College Street; tel: 416-531-7373; www.birreriavolo.com

Here you walk into a bare-brick alleyway with a ceiling, find a spot at the narrow bar, the summer patio or the communal seating at the back, and pick one of the 26 craft beers on tap. This is Little Italy's, if not the city's, coolest, industrial beer bar. Light bar snacks are available, too.

The Caledonian

856 College Street; tel: 416-577-7472; www.thecaledonian.ca

An inviting Scottish pub in Little Italy that boasts a huge whisky menu of over 300 malts and blends, plus special Scottish beers on tap. Of course, haggis is on the menu, as are Scotch eggs, fish and chips and meat pies.

CC Lounge & Whisky Bar

45 Front Street East; tel: 416-362-4777; www.cconfront.com

For whisky lovers, this vintage restaurant and bar, with a 1920s prohibition-

era decor, specializes in whiskeys – over 300 of them. You can also tour the on-site tunnel, built in 1891, which was used to facilitate the illegal trade and smuggling of prohibited spirits.

The Dakota Tavern

249 Ossington Avenue; tel: 416-850-4579; www.thedakotatavern.com

Long-standing local favourite dive bar, located in a basement, with a country vibe and nightly live music acts. Standard beers and drinks, and on the weekends the Bluegrass Brunch features a live band accompanied by a satisfying breakfast menu.

Drake Underground

1150 Queen Street West; tel: 416-531-5042; www.thedrake.ca

One of the top bars and music venues in the city, The Drake Hotel's subterranean space is constantly hopping with DJs, live indie music, movie screenings and comedy performances. You can also head upstairs to the lounge or rooftop patio of the hotel for a drink or bite to eat.

The Emmet Ray

924 College Street; tel: 416-792-4497; www.theemmetray.com

An inviting, classy bar with an extensive whisky list, elevated pub fare and nightly entertainment, including live music and stand-up comedy nights.

The Gaslight

1426 Bloor Street West; tel: 647-402-9728; www.thegaslightto.com

A warm and friendly candle-lit watering hole with church pews for seating and music just quiet enough to allow for good conversation. The drinks menu includes local wines, craft beers, and simple cocktails. A modest snack menu of comfort foods such as charcuterie boards and pizzas is on offer as well.

Handlebar

159 August Avenue; tel: 647-748-7433

For a local beer or simple whisky, plus homey and budget-friendly snacks, this intimate neighbourhood bar in Kensington Market has a lively karaoke night on Tuesdays, plus DJs spin retro tunes on weekends. Up-and-coming live music acts frequent the place as well.

Horseshoe Tavern

370 Queen Street West; tel: 416-598-4226; www.horseshoetavern.com

Legendary bar and music venue, dating back to the 1950s. Once upon a time big names, including Willie Nelson and Talking Heads have played here. Excellent live performances continue to this day, and the A&W take-out window is just plain fun.

King Taps

100 King Street West; tel: 647-361-2025; www.kingtaps.com

With over 50 beers on tap, this sprawling, two-story sports bar has an extensive pub food menu as well. The outdoor patios are packed during lunchtime,

Hair-raising Drake Underground

and there are big-screen TVs all over the place so you won't miss a game. Try the beer flights for a good selection, along with a wood-fired pizza.

Mahjong Bar

1276 Dundas Street West; tel: 647-980-5664; www.mahjongbar.com

Hidden behind a small, pink-painted convenience store, this stylish retro bar, with its soft red glow, serves fresh tropical cocktails, unusual beers, and delicate Chinese appetizers. Try the Green Dragon cocktail, made with gin, melon, lemon, and egg white, alongside the Mahjong Half Moon meat and vegetable pockets.

Mulberry Bar

828 Bloor Street West; www.mulberry.bar

Elegant, light-and-lush, plant-filled French-style cocktail bar with a pretty, street-side seasonal patio. The cocktails created here are dreamy and sophisticated, and the wines pair well with the imported cheeses.

The Shameful Tiki Room

1378 Queen Street West; www.shamefultikiroom.com

Decked out in bamboo and wicker, the low-lit, Polynesian atmosphere here is perfect for a fancy tropical cocktail or two. Try the Mystery Bowl drink, ideally for two or more people. The kitchen makes delicious snacks until the wee hours, including mini-burger sliders, fish tacos, deep fried crab wontons and chicken satay.

Three Speed

1163 Bloor Street West; tel: 647-430-3834

Friendly neighbourhood pub where the backyard-feel patio is the main attraction. It features an old fireplace, lush plants and plenty of locals. Come for a simple but satisfying brunch on weekends, or stay late for beers and sandwiches.

Toronto Movie Theatres

For a list of all movie theatres in Toronto, check out www.cinemaclock.com/ont/toronto/theatres.

Carlton Cinema

20 Carlton Street; tel: 416-598-5454; www.imaginecinemas.com

Old-school movie theatre from the early 80s, still going strong. It shows new Hollywood releases, second-run movies, plus independent and cult foreign movies.

The Fox Theatre

2236 Queen Street East; tel: 416-691-7335; www.foxtheatre.ca

Dating back to 1914, this vintage and restored, Beaches neighbourhood, single-screen movie theatre plays a mixture of second-run, independent and foreign movies, plus special event screenings. It's also licensed so you can have a drink with your popcorn.

Varsity Cinemas

55 Bloor Street; tel: 416-961-6304; www.cineplex.com

King Street West entertainment district at night

All the big blockbusters will be playing at this modern, multiplex theatre, so it's always buzzing with people. There's a VIP screen here as well, which is for adults only and allows for dinner and drinks to be served right to your seats.

Toronto Comedy Club

Comedy Bar
945 Bloor Street West; tel: 416-551-6540; www.comedybar.ca

Excellent, if sometimes off-beat, performers tell their best jokes in this modest space. Tickets are relatively inexpensive at this venue as new and upcoming talents are frequently on stage.

Toronto Nightclubs

Coda
794 Bathurst Street; tel: 416-536-0346; www.codatoronto.com

EDM (electronic dance music) enthusiasts flock in numbers to this sprawling, two-storey club near Koreatown This is where DJs pump up the volume on the weekends and club-goers relish in the deep sounds and flashing lights of the venue.

Wildflower
550 Wellington Street West; tel: 647-778-8462; www.loveusnot.com

Located downstairs, inside the slick Thompson Hotel, this sleek, modern lounge resembles a vast art gallery. DJs play all the top hits and its clientele are well dressed. The Thompson Hotel also has a chic rooftop lounge and pool for cocktails and sushi.

Toronto Jazz and Blues Bars

Poetry Jazz Café
224 Augusta Avenue; tel: 416-599-5299; www.poetryjazzcafe.com

Lively, casual, dimly-lit bar hidden behind graffiti-clad wooden sliding doors in the Kensington Market neighbourhood. Nightly live performances include experimental jazz, soul, funk and blues. Cocktails here are excellent as well, notably the Bitches Brew concocted with aged dark Caribbean rum, tequila, grapefruit, brown sugar, lime and spices.

The Reservoir Lounge
52 Wellington Street East; tel: 416-955-0887; www.reservoirlounge.com

Five nights a week a different band is playing a different sound, with a general jazz and blues theme, at this busy and intimate live music and dance lounge. And if you arrive here hungry, they make excellent pizzas too. A top venue all in all.

The Rex Hotel Jazz and Blues Bar
194 Queen Street West; tel: 416-598-2475; www.therex.ca

Since the early 1980s, The Rex has been part of the city's thriving local jazz scene. Every night there's a band on stage here, from local talent to world-

Four Seasons Centre for the Performing Arts

renowned musicians from across the globe.

See also the Entertainment section (see page 20). For the Elgin and Winter Garden Theatres, see page 29.

Ed Mirvish Theatre

244 Victoria Street; tel: 1-800-461-3333 (TicketKing); www.mirvish.com

First built in 1920, this historic film and play theatre shows big Broadway and London musicals. Guided tours can be arranged to take a closer look at the ornate and carefully restored interior.

Four Seasons Centre for the Performing Arts

145 Queen Street West; tel: 416-363-8231 (box office); www.coc.ca

Home to the Canadian Opera Company and the National Ballet of Canada, this modern structure was purpose-built for opera and ballet and features the finest level of acoustics. Something to note is that you can often get heavily discounted rush tickets that go on sale at 11am on the day of the performance; the Four Seasons also has a programme of free concerts (see website) for those on a budget.

Koerner Hall

273 Bloor Street West; tel: 416-408-0208; www.rcmusic.com

One of North America's most acoustically superb concert halls, and inside The Royal Conservatory of Music.

Phoenix Concert Theatre

410 Sherbourne St; tel: 416-323-1251; www.phoenixconcerttheatre.com

A lavish three-venue concert venue which specializes in booking big-name acts looking for intimate gigs. A range of artists from Sharon van Etten to Richard Thompson, Cesaria Evora and Green Day have performed here.

Roy Thomson Hall

60 Simcoe Street; tel: 416-872-4255 (box office); www.roythomsonhall.com

Designed by Canadian architect Arthur Erickson, this splendid circular building was built in the early 1980s to house the Toronto Symphony Orchestra and the Toronto Mendelssohn Choir. It is also one of the main venues for the Toronto International Film Festival (TIFF).

Chez Lucien

137 Murray Street at Dalhousie; tel: 613-241-3533

Smashing, Québec-style joint with a well-chosen selection of craft beers plus great burgers, escargot and a (free) jukebox.

The Manx

370 Elgin Street; tel: 613-231-2070; www.manxpub.com

Roy Thomson Hall

This basement pub packs the locals in tight with a boisterous crew having an energetic bash at all the twenty-odd beers on draught. Not for the faint-hearted.

Quinn's Ale House

1170 Bank St; tel: 613-523-2200; www.quinnsalehouse.com

Not much of a looker from the outside perhaps, however, this small and cozy bar is an amenable sort of place. Here you can find a range of impressive local and international draught beers on offer.

Rainbow Bistro

76 Murray Street; tel: 613-241-5123; www.therainbow.ca

Atmospheric blues and jazz club with regular jam sessions and good sidelines in reggae, funk, rock and ska. Open nightly.

Canadian Tire Centre

1000 Palladium Drive; tel: 613-599-3267; www.canadiantirecentre.com

Located approximately 15km west of downtown at Kanata, Canadian Tire Centre is Ottawa's big-deal concert arena which attracts big-name rock and pop acts. Previous performers have included a range of stars from Barbra Streisand to Madonna. In addition, the venue is home to the Ottawa Senators ice hockey team.

Great Canadian Theatre Company

1233 Wellington St West; tel: 613-236-5196; www.gctc.ca

A fantastic not-for-profit theatre company in the Hintonburg area. Here you can really make the most of an adventurous and vibrant programme with modern Canadian playwrights to the fore.

National Arts Centre

1 Elgin Street; tel: 1-844-985-2787 (box office); www.nac-cna.ca

This is Ottawa's cultural focus, presenting plays by its resident theatre company as well as touring groups, concerts by its resident orchestra, and opera and dance from (among others) the National Ballet of Canada and the Royal Winnipeg Ballet; the acoustics are outstanding here, it is well worth a visit.

Ottawa Little Theatre

400 King Edward Ave; tel: 613-233-8948; www.ottawalittletheatre.com

This is a fantastic top-of-the-range community theatre found in a downtown location. The theatre showcases a varied programme of performances which includes modern classics (and not-so-classics) which range from Agatha Christie and Noël Coward to Arthur Miller.

A selection at Indigo Bookstore

BOOKS AND FILM

Ontario in general and Toronto in particular have succoured a **literary scene** since the middle of the nineteenth century. Initially, most writers were more preoccupied with lofty discussions on matters of church and state, rather than the pastoral delights of Canadian life. Indeed, Toronto and Ontario as themes in Canadian literature only emerged after World War I, beginning with the small-town humourist Stephen Leacock. In the late 1950s and early 1960s, however, Toronto witnessed a remarkable flowering of prose, poetry, painting and theatre in which place – in this case Toronto and Ontario – was fundamental to storytelling. For them, and this included the most talented of them, Margaret Atwood, Toronto was not "a place to graduate from", but a place to stay. It was on this strong base that Toronto's literary scene has continued to blossom and, reflecting the changes to its population, diversify.

As for the film and television industry, Toronto is buzzing, buoyed by the skills of its film crews and its great locations. The city is – or has been – home to such series as *Designated Survivor, Suits, Star Trek: Discovery, The Handmaid's Tale* and many more. Director David Cronenberg (*Videodrome, eXistenZ, A History of Violence, Crash*) and comedian Howie Mandel (*Deal or No Deal*), both Torontonians, have helped shape both sides of the industry, too.

Fiction

The Blind Assassin by Margaret Atwood. A historical science fiction novel set in Toronto during the 1930s and 1940s.

What's Bred in the Bone by Robertson Davies. For many years the leading figure of Canada's literary scene, Davies, who died in 1995, wrote dark and complicated novels of familial history set in the semi-rural Ontario of his youth.

Cabbagetown by Hugh Garner. A young man faces the bleak prospects of the Great Depression in Toronto's Cabbagetown neighbourhood.

Roughing It in the Bush: or Life in Canada by Susanna Moodie. An intriguing novel that was written in 1852. The story describes an English couple's attempt to create a new life together which sees them in southeastern Ontario.

In the Skin of a Lion by Michael Ondaatje. A mystery and love story about immigrant life set in Toronto during the 1920s and 1930s.

Consolation by Michael Redhill. The story of two families in Toronto living centuries apart, with an unusual connection.

The Incomparable Atuk by Mordecai Richler. A satirical novel about a young Inuit man who moves to Toronto and learns to adapt to the ways of the big city.

Unless by Carol Shields. The final novel by Shields, this semi-autobiographical fictional story recalls the difficulties of a dysfunctional family living in Toronto.

Liberty Village Park outdoor summer movies

The Wives of Bath by Susan Swan. A Toronto girls' school in the Sixties is the setting for this novel written in a genre the author described as "sexual gothic".

Non-Fiction

No Mean City by Eric Arthur. A quintessential book on Toronto's architectural heritage and contemporary designs.

Toronto Between the Wars by Charles Cotter. Takes a look at the city between the period of World War I and World War II and includes 180 striking photographs.

Toronto: Biography of a City by Allan Levine. Explores four centuries of the city's history and its politics, ethnic diversity and overall development.

Toronto Then and Now by Doug Taylor. Coffee-table-style book that examines 75 heritage sites throughout the city and illustrates the changes that have taken place during the last century.

A Social History of Canada by George Woodcock. Erudite and incisive book about the peoples of Canada and the country's development.

Film and TV

Chloe, 2009. Toronto plays itself here in this well-received erotic thriller. The Allan Gardens, the Royal Ontario Museum, the CN Tower, and other recognizable sites are easily seen throughout the movie.

Dead Ringers, 1988. Directed by David Cronenberg, this thriller was set and filmed throughout the city, including various scenes at Casa Loma and Trinity Square Park.

Exotica, 1994. Canadian film director Atom Egoyan's breakthrough drama about a fictional strip club set in Toronto, with various shots featuring city landmark buildings such as the Metropolitan United Church and Osgoode Hall.

The Handmaid's Tale, 2017. Margaret Atwood's classic novel has now spawned four seasons of shows – and more may follow. Toronto locations are a key background feature of this dystopian tale.

Last Night, 1998. Torontonian Don McKellar directed this comedy drama, set and filmed in the city, about a group of people each facing the end of the world.

Owning Mahowny, 2003. Based on the true story of a Toronto bank manager who committed the largest bank fraud in Canadian history to feed his gambling habits.

Scott Pilgrim vs. the World, 2010. Based on a graphic novel series, this action comedy, entirely filmed in Toronto, is about a young musician who must battle seven evil exes of his new girlfriend.

The Shape of Water, 2017. Sci-fi paranoic tale with a splash of tenderness – and all filmed in and around Toronto.

Strange Brew, 1983. In this famous comedy based on SCTV (Second City Television – a Canadian sketch comedy show) characters, local actors Rick Moranis and Dave Thomas, who also served as a co-directors, get involved in a brewery mystery, with most film shots based in Toronto and its surrounding areas.

Videodrome, 1983. David Cronenberg's classic science-fiction horror flick set in Toronto during the early 1980s.

ABOUT THIS BOOK

This *Explore Guide* has been produced by the editors of Insight Guides, whose books have set the standard for visual travel guides since 1970. With top-quality photography and authoritative recommendations, these guidebooks bring you the very best routes and itineraries in the world's most exciting destinations.

BEST ROUTES

The routes in the book provide something to suit all budgets, tastes and trip lengths. As well as covering the destination's many classic attractions, the itineraries track lesser-known sights. The routes embrace a range of interests, so whether you are an art fan, a gourmet, a history buff or have kids to entertain, you will find an option to suit.

We recommend reading the whole of a route before setting out. This should help you to familiarise yourself with it and enable you to plan where to stop for refreshments – options are shown in the 'Food and Drink' box at the end of each tour.

For our pick of the tours by theme, consult Recommended Routes for… (see pages 6 – 7).

INTRODUCTION

The routes are set in context by this introductory section, giving an overview of the destination to set the scene, plus background information on food and drink, shopping and more.

DIRECTORY

Also supporting the routes is a Directory chapter, with our pick of where to stay while you are there and select restaurant listings; these eateries complement the more low-key cafés and restaurants that feature within the routes and are intended to offer a wider choice for evening dining. Also included here are some nightlife listings and our recommendations for books and films about the destination.

ABOUT THE AUTHOR

After training as a drama teacher many moons ago, Phil Lee switched to travel writing and has since written well over twenty Rough Guides, including those to Canada and Toronto. He has an abiding affection for Toronto and Ontario's Georgian Bay, where he wasted part of his youth before returning to his home town, Nottingham, in the UK.

CONTACT THE EDITORS

We hope you find this Explore Guide useful, interesting and a pleasure to read. If you have any questions or feedback on the text, pictures or maps, please do let us know. If you have noticed any errors or outdated facts, or have suggestions for places to include on the routes, we would be delighted to hear from you. Please drop us an email at hello@insightguides.com. Thanks!

CREDITS

Explore Toronto and Ontario
Editor: Zara Sekhavati
Author: Phil Lee
Head of DTP and Pre-Press: Rebeka Davies
Head of Publishing: Sarah Clark
Picture Editor: Tom Smyth & Michelle Bhatia
Cartography: Katie Bennett
Photo credits: Alamy 46; Christophe Jivraj
112; Chuck Ortiz 108; Destination Ontario
4ML, 4ML, 7T, 7MR, 7MR, 8MC, 8ML, 8MC,
8MR, 8MR, 8/9T, 18, 19L, 22, 26ML, 26MR,
76, 85, 86, 88; Destination Toronto 8ML, 14,
20, 23, 34, 50, 51, 58, 61L, 63L, 62/63,
63B, 65, 65B, 116, 119, 120, 123; Four
Seasons Hotels and Resorts 98MC, 98ML;
Hyatt 98ML, 100, 107; Igor Yu 101; iStock
4MC, 13, 48, 49, 55, 68; Jake Kivanc 110;
Jenna Marie Wakani 113; Kayla Rocca 17;
Khristel Stecher/Tourism Toronto 6ML;
Leonardo 102; LHW 98MR, 98MR, 98/99T;
Lisa Sakulensky Photography 30/31; Marriot
98MC, 103, 104; NearEMPTiness 95; Norm Li
/ Tourism Toronto 4MC; Shutterstock 1, 4MR,
4/5T, 6TL, 6MC, 6BC, 7M, 10, 11, 12, 15,
16, 18/19, 21, 24/25, 26MC, 26ML, 26MC,
26MR, 26/27T, 28, 29, 30, 31L, 32, 33, 35,
36, 37, 38, 39, 40/41, 42, 43, 44, 45, 47,
53L, 52/53, 53B, 54, 56, 57, 57B, 59, 60,
60/61, 62, 64, 66, 67, 69, 70, 71, 72/73,
74, 74B, 75L, 74/75, 77, 76B, 78, 79, 80,
81L, 80/81, 82, 83, 83B, 84, 84B, 87, 89,
90, 91, 92, 93, 94, 96, 97, 105, 115, 117,
121, 122; Stacey Brandford 109; Stuart Sakai
114; Tourism Toronto 4MR, 52; Vintage Hotels
106; www.tedchaiphotography.com 111; Zach
Slootsky 118
Cover credits: Toronto's financial-district
Shutterstock

Printed in China

DISTRIBUTION

UK, Ireland and Europe
Apa Publications (UK) Ltd
sales@insightguides.com
United States and Canada
Ingram Publisher Services
ips@ingramcontent.com
Australia and New Zealand
Booktopia
retailer@booktopia.com.au
Worldwide
Apa Publications (UK) Ltd
sales@insightguides.com

SPECIAL SALES, CONTENT LICENSING AND COPUBLISHING

Insight Guides can be purchased in bulk
quantities at discounted prices. We can create
special editions, personalised jackets and
corporate imprints tailored to your needs.
sales@insightguides.com
www.insightguides.biz

INDEX

MAP LEGEND

● Start of tour

→ Tour & route direction

❶ Recommended sight

❷ Recommended
    restaurant/café

★ Place of interest

❶ Tourist information

✈✈ Airport / Airfield

— — · Ferry route

Ⓜ Subway station - Toronto

Ⓢ Streetcar - Toronto

Ⓞ O-Train - Ottawa

🚌 Main bus station

Ⓜ Museum

𝟏 Statue/monument

✚ Church

☾ Mosque

📖 Library

🎭 Theatre

✉ Main post office

⊕ Hospital

🗼 Lighthouse

⚓ Beach

✳ Viewpoint

Park

Important building

Urban area

Transport hub

National park